Beyond COBOL
SURVIVAL IN BUSINESS
APPLICATIONS PROGRAMMING

GARY D. BROWN

A WILEY-INTERSCIENCE PUBLICATION

JOHN WILEY & SONS

New York • Chichester • Brisbane • Toronto

Library of Congress Cataloging in Publication Data:

Brown, Gary DeWard.
    Beyond COBOL.

    "A Wiley-Interscience publication."
    Includes index.
    1. Business—Data processing. 2. Electronic
digital computers—Programming. 3. COBOL
(Computer program language) I. Title.

HF5548.2.B7618   658'.05424   80-28650

Printed in the United States of America

10 9 8 7 6 5 4 3 2 1

Preface

Your first job as a business applications programmer is the most difficult one. Imagine yourself on your initial day of work. Everyone in the entire company knows what they are to be doing except you. Other people are blithely solving problems while your biggest success is locating the coffee machine. You could use some help.

I intend this book to give you a preview of the work you will be doing, the techniques you will need to use, and the environment in which you will work. It is a book of practical techniques—the techniques that will enable you to translate the idea for a system as received from a user or systems analyst, into working programs. Some knowledge of a programming language, preferably COBOL, is assumed, and you should have a general knowledge of computers and computer operating systems.

The book may be used as a supplementary text for an applications programming class. But primarily it is intended for independent study to improve your general skills.

This is the third in a series of books for business applications programmers that I have written. The first, *System/370 Job Control Language*, describes the facilities provided by the computer operating system, including I/O hardware and access methods, JCL, linkage editor, SORT/MERGE, and the utility programs. The second, *Advanced ANS COBOL with Structured Programming*, describes the full facilities of COBOL, with simple examples of their use. And this, the third, describes how you put everything together to solve problems.

My special thanks go to Richard Tracy from whom I learned so many of the business applications programming techniques, and whose down-to-earth experience in data processing has so often kept me on the track.

GARY D. BROWN

Los Angeles, California
March 1981

Contents

ONE

Introduction

YOUR FIRST JOB

There is a large gap between the computer science curriculum taught at universities and the applications programming done in business. It is not that the latter is the "real world" and the former is not; both are the real world. It is simply that your real world as a student is rudely terminated by graduation, and, driven by a prosaic desire to eat and to buy fancy cars, you resign yourself to a job.

Businesses have an insatiable appetite for application programmers, and since it is here that a disproportionately large number of graduates will find their first jobs, it is here that you will, too. It will be challenging, demanding, rewarding work, but it will little resemble the data processing taught in university courses. You arrive brimming with algorithms, recursive techniques, microprogramming applications, and methods for parsing syntax, but then you are required to do maintenance.

But it will turn out that the work you do in maintenance will be among your most valuable. You will quickly learn a great deal, both good and bad, by examining other people's programs. Maintenance also gives you a chance to exercise almost all your programming skills, including analysis, debugging, testing, writing code, documentation, and dealing with users.

As a business applications programmer, you will mostly work on projects by yourself or with one or two others. Teams of programmers working on immense projects are relatively rare; the usual case is a single person working on several small projects. At first you will, of course, be spending much of your time on maintenance. There will also be occasional conversions to a new computer or operating system, installation of package systems, and making additions to existing systems. Sooner or later you will talk with users to determine their needs, do analysis, design, program, debug, and place programs into production. The work will likely involve both programming and systems analysis.

What will the first couple of years be like? The quintessential first task will be to maintain a payroll system originally written back when computers had vacuum tubes and you could separate male and female employees by sorting on the salary. There will be scant documentation on the system, and what there is will seem as if written by a dropout from Neanderthal school. You will have to document it, a job that ranks in enjoyment slightly below standing in line to renew your driver's license.

Soon you will receive your first midnight call. It will be a computer operator, and the conversation will go something like this:

"The payroll system blew up again," the operator will say with unappropriate cheerfulness.

"Huh," you answer sleepily.

"Yea, you must have done something to the program," he says accusingly.

"Huh," you answer innocently.

"Well, you better drag yourself in here. My check is in that payroll, and if I don't get it on time, I'll lose my house, my car, and a day at the race track," he says menacingly.

"Huh," you answer, sympathetically.

Although you find the operator's personal problems unconvincing, you realize that others in the company, including the president, your boss, and yourself, depend on getting their payroll checks on time. And so you quickly make the 30 mile drive into work and try to fix the problem. With some luck you discover that a payroll clerk coded "b1" instead of "01" in a numeric field. This completely nonessential data item has caused the payroll to be late and put you a leg up on developing an ulcer. By morning you are well on your way to becoming an applications programmer.

The company will finally decide to replace the antiquated payroll system with a new one. While you hope to participate in the design of a new system, the company will instead purchase a payroll package and give you two months in which to install it. This will seem reasonable to you because the coding, debugging, and documentation are already done, and all you have to do is implement it. No big deal.

Eight months later when the system is finally implemented, you will begin to understand how difficult the task has been. You will have found that what you saved in not designing the system you spent in learning it, in attempting to change it to your company's needs, in converting from the old system to the new one, in training users, and in getting a few bugs out of the system that were caused by a new version of the operating system. You will discover that implementing the package took longer than you estimated to write the payroll system from scratch. But the company will still be ahead because it would probably have taken you three times as long to write the payroll system as you estimated. You will have learned that there is much more to programming than coding.

But the real challenge will come when you must deal with customers in designing a new system. (Customers are people requesting your services;

they are usually in other departments within your company.) People tend to view the computer as a problem solver. This makes the computer seem to have a sedative effect on problems. In fact, it has a stimulative effect. The computer is a catalyst. You may sit down with a customer to go over a request for a program that is wanted. Then you go away to program it and bring back a report containing real life data. The customer will look it over, and then things begin to click in his mind.

"Say, this is great," he says. "I wonder, could you move these two columns together?"

"Oh sure," you say, "That's not difficult."

"Good, and could we also add a column for year-to-date amounts?"

"Yes, I suppose so," you say, "but I will have to redesign the report because there is not enough space on the page for more columns."

"Great, and could we print the last year-to-date amounts too?"

"I guess so," you say with decreasing enthusiasm. "It only means redesigning the entire system in order to maintain the last year-to-date amounts."

"Fine, fine. When you get that, I'd like to see it again."

In five minutes the customer has laid out six months of work for a minor project you thought you had finished. All of this is to point out a theme of this book. Business applications programming is difficult. As a seasoned manager once remarked, "You don't do anything in computing without bleeding."

Why is programming so difficult? There are several reasons. First, a computer program consists of perhaps a few hundred statements, and a computer system can contain from 20,000 to 100,000 statements. If we use an analogy with a mechanical system, each statement can be thought of as a moving part. For the system to operate properly, each statement must perform correctly. It does not take much imagination to visualize the potential for error in putting together a machine with 100,000 moving parts. Even after exhaustive debugging, any system is bound to have latent errors waiting only to occur when they can do the most damage.

You may concede that this makes the system difficult to debug; but once debugged, shouldn't the computer's hardware reliability ensure that the statements will operate the same each time they are executed? Here you might argue that the analogy with a mechanical system breaks down. Mechanical systems are subject to physical wear and require maintenance. Computer systems are not.

Wrong! It is not that the computer statements wear out. It is just that their function wears out. The needs change. Also, each time the system is run, it encounters different data and different combinations of data. Latent bugs move to the surface, unplanned combinations of events occur, and even physical storage capacities are exceeded. The unpredictable becomes commonplace.

For example, a new company policy to give maternity leave to husbands would raise havoc in a payroll system in which, to save space in the records, maternity leave for women was stored in the same area of the record that was used to record the draft status for men. Registering women for the draft would cause a similar problem.

The ugly truth is that computer systems are inherently inflexible. This may come somewhat as a surprise because so much emphasis is placed on making computer programs flexible. We forget that the reason so much effort is put into this is because they are inherently inflexible. Granted, computers can be programmed to handle an amazing range of problems, but once programmed, they are as difficult to change as a bad habit. Again, the analogy with the mechanical system makes this more understandable. If someone tells you that he has a machine with 100,000 moving parts and he is going to make a few "minor" changes, you know that he will be lucky if the contraption ever runs again.

The fact that data is retained over time also makes business data processing harder. When a problem occurs, it is not enough to correct the program. You must also correct the files should bad data get into them. If a file is changed, all the programs that access the file may have to be modified. This introduces considerable inertia into making changes.

The long life of business programs makes it likely that if there are latent bugs, someday they will come to light. And the longer the life, the more likely that the program will have to be changed. There is time for documentation to become obsolete, for source listings and even source decks to be lost, and for the program's original author to skip to South America after making some mysterious changes to the accounts payable system.

The sheer size of business systems is a problem. It is not unusual for a system to run for hours. The extended time on the computer exposes it to hardware and operating system problems. The system may also exceed some physical limitation, such as the amount of data that can be stored on a tape reel or disk. It is very difficult to track down data problems that occur a couple of hours into a run. Rescheduling or rerunning long jobs may be possible, but only if you have no scruples about bribing the scheduler. You must give careful attention to backing up files and being able to restart programs in the event that something goes wrong.

And then there is change. We live on the residual debris of the gigantic explosion that formed the universe. Traveling through space at millions of miles an hour, our earth lies at the edge of an otherwise nondescript galaxy where suns are born from congealed energy and die into black holes. The thrusting plates of our drifting continents expose the fossils of untold species that were evolved and became extinct. And yet, change always seems to take us by surprise—as if it were outside the natural order of things.

As an example of the impact of change, a company was planning its third management information system. Because the first two were utter disasters, the company made every effort to ensure its success. It formed a committee of users who were made a part of the design group. The company's president and top management, in addition to giving their full support, became intimately involved with the project. Before implementing the system, the design group made a dry run in which reports were prepared by hand from actual data and distributed to the managers. The design group also made a special flexibility study to determine the effect of likely changes during the life of the system.

Then the system was installed. The users reacted with complete surprise, as if it were being forced on them by alien beings. In six months much of the system had been changed. And yet the effort was worthwhile. Most management information systems fail completely, and since this system worked and most users were only mildly hostile to it, it has to be considered a fantastic success.

And the flexibility study? The changes that actually occurred were not anticipated in the study. For example, the system was run weekly, and no one questioned that there would be other than 52 weeks in a year. And yet the system ran for three years before it had a 52 week year. The first year the company changed from a calendar fiscal year to the government's fiscal year ending in June. This resulted in a 26 week year. Then the government changed the end of its fiscal year to September, necessitating a 65 week fiscal year.

The lesson is not that a flexibility study is a bad idea; it is that you will never be able to anticipate all the changes that might occur in any system. Good programmers have learned humility—if not paranoia. Never underestimate the catalytic effect of data. Almost any system you work on will be changed during its development, it will take longer than planned, and the customer will never be entirely satisfied with the results. Systems are never completed. Eventually a point is reached where no one is willing to pay for all the things that remain to be done.

THE CUSTOMERS

Directly or indirectly you will be working with two main groups of customers: accounting and operations. Accounting systems, such as general ledger, accounts receivable, and personnel/payroll, must satisfy legal as well as corporate requirements, in accordance with generally accepted accounting practices. The accounting needs, while important, do not directly help the company produce its product.

Operations might include sales, research, marketing, production, engineering, corporate management, and whatever else the company does. Managers can use the computer as a direct aid in producing their product. Automated design and bill of materials processing are examples of this, but the most common use of the computer by managers is to obtain information for making decisions. The information may not correspond to legal or accounting requirements, or to generally accepted accounting principles. Consequently the data needed by management will differ from the data needed by accounting. Accounting is interested in things quantifiable in dollars, whereas management is interested not only in costs, but also in units of production, sales, head counts, and hours. Functions such as scheduling, quality control, and order entry may require data different from that required for accounting, or at least organized and presented differently.

For example, accounting might not care how salespeople rank in sales, but a manager would. Likewise, a manager may want to see a cost reported as a commitment as soon as a decision has been made to spend the money, whereas accounting may want to record costs only when they have been vouchered.

The needs of operating managers and the financial division of a company often conflict, and the question of where computing should report is controversial. If placed under financial control, accounting needs can be served at the expense of operational needs, and the reverse occurs when it is placed under operational control.

You as a programmer may not get caught up in the conflict, but you will get caught up in the needs. Operational needs are often more complicated than accounting needs. They require more data, a more sophisticated presentation, and there are no generally accepted accounting practices upon which to standardize.

Your most difficult task in working with customers is to get them to settle on what they want. A brilliantly designed, coded, tested, and documented system is for naught unless it does what the customers want. Your first challenge is then to help make the customers know what they want. This sometimes requires skillful diplomacy and persuasion when they want something not possible or not in their best interest. Then you must lead them to an acceptable alternative.

The next most important thing is that you understand what the customers want. You should establish a relationship with them to secure their trust and enable you to obtain from them all the monumental detail required for a computer application. As much as you can, you should make the customers a part of the project team. This puts them on your side, and it gives them a proprietary interest in the system's development. By getting the customers to concentrate on what they need and how they will be impacted when the system goes into operation, you lessen the probability of changes after the system is implemented. This is critical because a change during the design phase that might take half a day could take six months to make after the system is implemented.

One way to involve the customers in the project is to make periodic presentations to them. You can review the system design, discussing the inputs, processing, and reports. You might go over the run schedule of the implemented system and point out what will be required from various people in the organization. You can also go over the project's schedule and where you are in the implementation. You might point out the sensitivity of the schedule to design changes. Not only does this keep the customers interested and up to date on the project, but it also forces you to keep the customers' needs in mind. Knowing that you must make presentations of the system to the customers makes you do a better job.

PROGRAMMING TOOLS

In your first job you will find that job control language, or JCL (if you work on an IBM computer, which you probably will), the utility programs, and the sort package are your constant tools. FORTRAN, PL/I, Pascal, and APL will give way almost entirely to COBOL. This is not to say that the others are poor languages—in many ways they are better than COBOL— but COBOL is the language of business applications.

COBOL has two major advantages. First, while it may be tedious to write, it is relatively easy to read. This is important because you will be reading programs more than you will be writing them. Second, COBOL is excellent at specifying data in records and files, and business applications are predominantly the maintenance of data. In fact, you will consider yourself lucky when you are able to write programs in COBOL. Often the task will be to implement or maintain a package system. And increasingly, you may be using a nonprocedural language in which you check boxes on a form rather than write language statements.

Nonprocedural languages and package systems partly reflect the concern over programmer productivity. Since the early 1960s when higher level languages such as COBOL came into wide use, programmer productivity has stayed relatively constant. This stable productivity looks particularly unfavorable when contrasted with hardware productivity in which there has been roughly a tenfold increase in cost/performance each decade.

This gap between hardware and programmer productivity has led to an intense search for better programming techniques, such as modular programming, structured programming, and top-down programming. Many of the new techniques do help, although none have had a significant effect on overall productivity. The early enthusiasm leads to disappointment when these techniques prove not to be panaceas, and the disappointment sometimes masks the fact that they do help.

And the new programming techniques do help. Some of the benefits accrue only when an entire installation has adopted them and undergone intense training. And then it is never clear whether the gains result from the attention paid to training, from the consistency in the programming techniques that result, or from the fact that people often do better when they are expected to. A large part of the benefit may also come from the attention paid to better ways to design and program. It seems reasonable that if we are made to recognize good and bad ways to program, there is an opportunity to become better.

Of the new techniques, structured programming and top-down design have had the most attention. Structured programming limits the control statements in a program, forcing you to code sequentially rather than jumping all around. By using fewer control statements, programs become more consistent. Top-down design requires you to have an overall structure in mind before you get immersed in detail, and it is easy to be so buried in details that you fail to organize the overall structure of your program into something that makes sense. Top-down design also helps you to isolate functions within a program, with the result that things belonging together are placed together. This makes the interfaces between parts of programs much cleaner, which in turn makes programs more understandable and easier to change. Both structured programming and top-down design are employed in this book, without emphasizing the fact that they are being used.

Some of the new techniques fall short because they demand too much from the programmer. Structured walkthroughs are such an example. In a proper structured walkthrough, a group of about six programmers spend an hour per session to discuss perhaps 100 lines of code in a program. The weakness of the structured walkthrough is that it is so difficult to organize, manage, and sustain that it becomes a dominant problem in itself.

Another reason for the failure of some new techniques is that they fall prey to what might be termed the "Michelangelo" syndrome. That is, if you want to paint your ceiling, the best way is to hire a Michelangelo and give him 11 years to complete the job. Unfortunately the world is populated with few Michelangelos, and should you find one, he is unlikely to want to paint your miserable little ceiling. Chief programming teams, in which one superior programmer is supported by a small team, fall prey to this weakness. There are not enough superior programmers to go around.

Techniques that require an inordinate effort and superhuman dedication have limited use. We pay lip service to such techniques, but little else. They are like the advice we have probably all heard, to chew each bite of food 30 times before swallowing. Yes, we all should, but who does? Would you even like to dine with someone who did?

While the discrepancy between hardware and programmer productivity will remain, the hardware productivity can help programmer productivity. In programming there is often a tradeoff between hardware costs and programming costs. Obviously, as hardware performance increases with decreasing costs, and programming costs increase with constant productivity, it becomes more and more effective to use hardware when it saves programmer time. For example, large programs will run more efficiently if written in assembler language, but can be coded faster in COBOL. Given the spectacular increases in hardware cost/performance, there should be little reason for using assembler language today for efficiency. Text editors and remote job entry terminals exchange hardware costs for faster turnaround time. Syntax errors can be found by a compilation run if this is less expensive than finding them by hand.

Because of the increasingly favorable tradeoff of hardware for programmer effort, you will more and more come into contact with package systems and nonprocedural languages. Both are generally less efficient than custom programs written in COBOL, but both require less programming effort. With a nonprocedural language, such as RPG, MARK IV, or DYL260, you do not direct the computer with step-by-step procedures or language statements. Instead you code specifications for the program, generally with a coding form, and a compiler generates the program.

While there are significant advantages in the time required to write programs, there are some disadvantages. None of the nonprocedural languages is as well known as COBOL, and you may first have to learn the language to write programs or maintain them. There will also be fewer people who know the language and can help you when you encounter problems. Unfortunately, while nonprocedural languages are easier to write than COBOL, they are more difficult to read. A single character in a field can result in loading a table, but when you read the program, all you see is a single character in a particular column. COBOL would require several statements to read in a table, but you can read the program and see that a table is being read. Nonprocedural languages are less powerful than COBOL, and this limits their use.

Package systems are general purpose application programs, such as a payroll or accounts receivable package. Rather than program, you select options and tailor the package to your needs. The advantage is that they require little programming effort. As general purpose applications, they may provide features that would be prohibitive for you to program, and they may contain facilities to accommodate an unexpected or future requirement. Packages generally come with application and software support, documentation, manuals, forms, and reports.

They too have several disadvantages. The quality differs with the various packages and with the vendors. The strength of packages is also their weakness. It takes relatively little effort to obtain what is provided by the package. It can take inordinate effort to obtain what is not provided by the package.

Packages are difficult to modify. If extensive modifications are needed, you are better off not using a package. The success of a package system is determined more by the selection than by anything else. Packages are unsuited where the needs are not well known in advance. As a result, package systems work best in standard applications, such as payroll, personnel, general ledger, inventory, accounts receivable, and accounts payable. They are less successful where the needs vary widely among companies, such as for management information systems.

In addition to nonprocedural languages and package systems, the next decade will likely see improvements in programming tools. As with any profession, improved tools lead to improved productivity. There was a quantum leap when COBOL was introduced as a programming tool in the early 1960s. Another quantum leap occurred in the mid-1960s with job control language and improvements in the computer's operating system. Online systems, text editors, sort packages, utility programs, report writers, and data base systems have all made their contributions, and we can expect to see more.

PROJECTS

In addition to maintenance, you will have the opportunity to work on projects in developing new systems. Regardless of their size, most projects have a similar life cycle consisting of discrete steps. Generally there is some plan at the beginning and a review at the end of each step. The extent and formality of the plan and review depend upon the size of the project. Large projects may require a formal presentation with a written summary. For a small project you may plan and review for yourself.

The first step in the cycle is to develop the need for the system. It may be at the request of a customer, or you as an analyst may see the need. However it occurs, the requirements need to be thought out and agreed upon by those concerned. The goal is to describe what is to be accomplished, and this usually requires working with the customer.

The next step in the cycle is an overall design, and this involves considerable analysis. Usually this design will not go into deep detail on how to program the system, but will lay out the general approach. Various people will need to review it to see that it meets the requirements, that it can be afforded, that people are available to do it, and that it can be done within a reasonable period of time.

After the preliminary design, the cycle continues with the detailed design. This is directed toward the programmer. It will include file layouts, program specifications, standards and conventions, report layouts, and the programming tools to use.

Coding comes next in the cycle, and may even begin before the entire design is complete. And with coding comes testing. Each program or portion of a program is usually tested after it is written.

Systems testing becomes a separate step in the cycle after all the individual pieces have been tested. When they are put together, all the interface problems occur. The system now begins to produce output that means something to users. Hence they may become involved at this stage to verify the results and to begin the training for the new system.

After systems testing and verification, the implementation step begins. This may require training users, preparing user manuals, converting files, setting up production JCL, preparing run documentation, training a run group, and planning the timing of the installation. This is the period of maximum effort and anxiety in the life cycle. Usually the system will be replacing an old one, requiring a conversion, perhaps a parallel run, and a cutover.

After the system is installed and operational, there should be a post-mortem. It is good to step back and summarize the problems, reflect on what was learned, what could have been done better, what could have been omitted, and what should be done later. This postproject review is an important learning process, and you should do it even if you do it only for yourself. If nothing else, it may help you write your résumé.

The final phase in the life cycle is maintenance. Errors will occur, changes will develop, and the system will need mothering. Maintenance continues until the system ages to where it must be replaced, and the entire cycle repeats.

THE PLAN OF THIS BOOK

No book can cover everything that you might encounter in business applications programming, but there are common threads running through most applications, whether they be a payroll system, a billing system, an accounts receivable system, an inventory system, or a manufacturing system. These common threads ultimately boil down to six processes.

1 **Collecting data** This involves getting the data from its original source, arranging it into the proper format, and storing it within a record in a file.

2 **Validation** Input data, like everything else in this world, is never perfect, and you must detect bad data to correct it, to keep it out of the files, and to keep it from causing a program to fail.

3 **Updating** Generally the input data consists of transactions that must be applied to a master file. Records must be added, deleted, or changed.

4 **Selecting and summarizing** For reporting or further processing you will often need to select the required data and summarize it.

5 **Sorting** Most updating, summarizing, and reporting require the data to be in some logical order.

6 **Reporting** The ultimate reason for collecting data is to generate reports from it.

Much of this book is spent on these six items since they constitute the heart of business applications programming. These topics are covered in the first eleven chapters, expanding on the techniques and problems that occur in business systems. On-line systems are described in Chapter 12. Chapter 13 describes documentation, which is the mortar that holds applications together. Chapter 14 concludes with maintenance, that enormous task which begins at the point where you think all your work is done.

Most of the book is slanted toward COBOL, although the PL/I programmer will have no difficulty in following the text. (The FORTRAN programmer had better learn COBOL, if only for job security.) Because nonprocedural languages and package systems are becoming increasingly important, the techniques in this book are related to them also.

The book is directed toward small projects because they permit more individual initiative than vast projects where your role is restricted. Also, most projects in industry are relatively small. The emphasis is on the functional needs of the job, which sometimes differ from what is conventionally expected. There is an abhorrence of unncessary work, and the book tries to steer you away from it.

TWO

Data in Business Applications

In this chapter we examine the types of data provided by the computer and the problems likely to be encountered in operations on the data. We also analyze the functional types of data used in business applications, such as dates, names, and hours, and give examples of the operations performed on them.

In business applications, information consists of entities and attributes. An entity is an item, such as a general ledger account number, which has attributes, such as asset or liability, which describe it. You need to think about data in these terms because it will help you structure the data. In a record, the record key is the entity and the remaining data in the record are the attributes.

Data representation is classified in two ways for business applications: numeric and nonnumeric. Because COBOL is the basic language of business applications, the data is described here in COBOL terms. Also, the IBM COBOL implementation is assumed for machine dependent data.

NONNUMERIC DATA

Nonnumeric Data Types

COBOL subdivides nonnumeric data into alphanumeric and alphabetic. The smallest unit of data is a character, it occupies a byte of storage, 8 bits on most computers. Alphanumeric data (PIC X in COBOL) can contain any character in the computer's character set. Alphabetic data (PIC A in COBOL) can contain only the characters A–Z and blank. However, most compilers treat alphabetic data the same as alphanumeric data—surprisingly few data items contain only alphabetic characters anyway. Names such as O'Neill contain nonalphabetic characters. In practice there are few reasons for using alphabetic data—use alphanumeric.

Nonnumeric data is used for data that identifies and classifies, such as names and addresses. Arithmetic operations cannot be performed on it. The major problem with nonnumeric data is to determine the length of the field. You must allocate the maximum field size that the data can contain, and this can be difficult. How many characters should be allocated for a name? Suggested field sizes are given later in this chapter.

Nonnumeric Data Problems

Name Fields   A person's name carried in a file often participates in a sort and is also printed. These two operations conflict because we usually sort last name first and print in the reverse order. If the name is stored as three separate alphanumeric data items, last, middle, and first name, it can be sorted last name first, but the name will be printed with irregular spaces because of the blanks allowed for the maximum name size.

DOE	JOHN	THOMAS

[As stored]

JOHN	THOMAS	DOE

[As it would be printed, one field at a time]

The simplest solution is to print only the first and middle initials in the name. Since they are a single character each, the blanks present no problem. The name would be printed as:

J. T. DOE

If the full name must be printed, there are two ways. The first method is to carry the name twice in the file, once for sorting and once for printing.

DOE	JOHN	THOMAS

[For sorting]

JOHN T. DOE

[For printing]

This is often the best solution because it is easy and allows you to sort on names that follow a sorting convention different from that of the computer. For example, the convention is to sort Mc Call as if it were spelled MCCALL and D'Arc as if it were spelled DARC. The disadvantage is that it requires more data entry time and storage space.

The other way is to write the statements necessary to edit out the blanks so that the names appear as they should. Unfortunately this is different to do in COBOL, except with the STRING verb. This is an excellent example of the unexpected complexity of seemingly simple business applications.

In a COBOL compiler without the STRING verb, some extensive programming is required. The data item to receive the formatted name must be described as a table in which each table element is a single character. Each name, first, middle, and last, must also be redefined as tables in which each element is a single character. Then you examine the first name, a character at a time, and move the character to the print name if it is nonblank, incrementing an index into the formatted name table. When you encounter two consecutive blanks, you stop. The reason for terminating on two blanks rather than on one is to avoid making enemies of the MC DONALDs, VON HAGENs, and VAN DYKEs.

The STRING verb available in some COBOL compilers considerably simplifies formatting names. It searches an alphanumeric data item until delimited by the encounter of specified characters, and moves all the characters up to the delimiter into a receiving field. It also updates a pointer into the receiving field so that you can move blanks in to separate the names. The following STRING verb would perform the formatting, and is included to show the power of some of the newer COBOL language features:

```
77  CURRENT-POSITION      PIC S9(4) COMP.
          □   □
    MOVE SPACES TO formatted-name.
    MOVE 1 TO CURRENT-POSITION.
    STRING first-name DELIMITED "bb" INTO formatted-name
                  POINTER CURRENT-POSITION
          "b" DELIMITED SIZE INTO formatted-name
                  POINTER CURRENT-POSITION
          middle-name DELIMITED "bb" INTO formatted-name
                  POINTER CURRENT-POSITION
          "b" DELIMITED SIZE INTO formatted-name
                  POINTER CURRENT-POSITION
          last-name DELIMITED "bb" INTO formatted-name
                  POINTER CURRENT-POSITION.
```

Coding Schemes When setting up a coding scheme, such as one for part numbers, the codes can serve to define the item. For example, if we were making up a code for toothpaste, the first two digits might indicate the size of the tube, the third the color, the fourth the flavor, and the last two the price. Selecting codes that are readily understood by the people who use them reduces error. For example, a part number of 10GC79 could easily be recognized as a 10 ounce tube of green colored, chocolate flavored toothpaste priced at 79¢—in other words, your basic 79¢ mint chocolate toothpaste.

The advantage of including attributes as part of the coding scheme is that the coding by itself can convey many of the attributes without reference to other sources. When the user of the code needs this information, including it as part of the coding scheme is very convenient. The problem with codes comes when the attributes that are built into the code can change. Green will still be green next year, but a 79¢ tube of toothpaste is likely to cost $3.85. Where the attributes can change, they should be given arbitrary values as table references. The price would have been better if coded as 02, and the 02 used as a reference to a table in which the current price is stored.

Hierarchical Data   Hierarchical data is common in business systems. The organization of a company is itself a hierarchy, and this hierarchy is often used in computer systems to generate reports. Figure 1 shows a typical organization chart in which the first level might represent a division, the second a department, and the third a group.

One way to represent a hierarchy or tree structure is to assign a number to each unit and let the numbers themselves specify the hierarchy. In Figure 1 the first digit could represent the division, the second digit the department, and the third digit the group. Now the hierarchy can be represented as a table as follows:

Organization Unit	Organization Name
100	Consumer Division
110	Production Department
111	Machine Shop
112	Assembly
120	Sales Department
.	
.	
.	

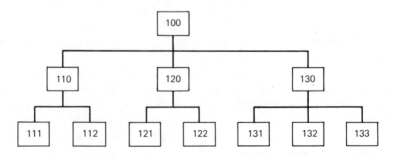

Figure 1   Company organization chart.

Sorting on the organization units arranges them in hierarchical order. The problem with letting the identifying numbers specify the hierarchy is that either we run out of numbers or we need to change the hierarchy. What happens if we need to transfer group 111 to be under department 120? We could assign it a new number such as 123, but this would be a major change. A better way is to store the hierarchy in a table as data:

Organization Unit	Level	Upward Hierarchy	Organization Name
100	1	100	Consumer Division
110	2	100 110	Production Department
111	3	100 110 111	Machine Shop
112	3	100 110 112	Assembly
120	2	100 120	Sales Department
.			
.			
.			

Sorting on the upward hierarchy places the table in hierarchical order. Since the numbers no longer specify the hierarchy, we can change the hierarchy by changing the table and not the organization number. Group 111 can be transferred under department 120 by changing the record in the table for group 111 as follows:

111	3	100 120 111	Machine Shop

The full hierarchy is often carried in cost records to group them together for reporting. To reduce the coding effort and minimize the chance for error, only the lowest level of organization is entered on a source transaction, and the hierarchy is looked up in a table during processing.

This leads to the problem of just when to look up the hierarchy. If the organization is looked up when the transaction is first processed, and carried in the cost records thereafter, changing the organization table will not change the hierarchy in existing records. That is, if group 111, which belonged to department 110, is transferred to department 120 by changing the organization table, old records containing the hierarchy will still show group 111 as belonging to department 110. If instead the hierarchy is looked up at report time, even old records will show groups as belonging to their current hierarchy. This in effect rewrites the cost history.

As a rule, accountants do not like to rewrite cost history, but operating managers do. Accountants would prefer to back the costs out and reenter them with journal entries so that they have an audit trail, rather than trusting the computer to do this automatically. But the journal entries will not satisfy managers, because they will want to see the full detail of the cost history, the budgets, and the labor reports follow the current organization. The accountant may be satisfied with a few journal entries to transfer costs by account, but the managers may want the costs by account by person by pay period to be transferred, and this is too burdensome to do with journal entries. A solution is to infer the hierarchy at input time for accounting reports, but reinfer the hierarchy just prior to sorting and reporting for management reports.

NUMERIC DATA

Numeric Data Types

Depending on the compiler, numeric data in COBOL can be numeric character (DISPLAY), binary (COMP), single precision, floating point (COMP-1), double precision, floating point (COMP-2), and packed decimal (COMP-3). Arithmetic operations can be performed on the data, and the data can be signed. Always make numeric data signed, even if the values are expected to be positive. Somehow you always end up needing numbers to contain negative values.

DISPLAY (Numeric-Character) Numbers   Numeric-character data is used for source input of numeric data and for numeric fields in reports. (Unlike many languages such as FORTRAN, COBOL cannot do data conversion on input or output.) A fixed number of digits to the left and right of an assumed decimal point are specified for the number.

Numeric-character data is relatively inefficient for arithmetic operations because the compiler must convert it to packed decimal or binary before performing the operation. For this reason, numeric-character data is often converted to COMP-3 for internal processing and storage in files.

COMP-1 and COMP-2 (Floating-Point) Numbers   COMP-1 and COMP-2 floating-point numbers are often used in scientific computations, but rarely in business applications. The number is stored in two parts: an exponent that determines the magnitude of the number, and a mantissa that contains the significant digits of the number. The advantage of floating-point data is that it permits arithmetic operations on numbers with a wide range of magnitudes. For example, 0.15436×10^6 times 0.54361×10^{-2} would yield 0.83812×10^3 if five significant digits of precision were maintained.

COMP-1 is single precision, usually five significant digits, and COMP-2 is double precision. Floating-point data is seldom used for business applications because they must balance to the penny rather than to some number of significant digits.

COMP (Binary) Numbers   COMP numbers are binary, and are the most efficient for arithmetic operations because the computer is a binary machine. However, they work best as internal integer counters and subscripts. The conversion from binary to digital with some number of digits to the left and right of an assumed decimal point gets complicated, and their inclusion in I/O records causes alignment problems. Generally COMP-3 works better.

COMP-3 (Packed-Decimal) Numbers   COMP-3 numbers are stored in the computer with each half byte (4 bits) representing a digit. Like numeric-character data, a fixed number of digits to the left and right of an assumed decimal point are specified for the number. COMP-3 data is not a part of ANS COBOL, but was designed into the hardware of many computers to meet the needs of business applications. COMP-3 data is relatively efficient for computations, easily converts to numeric-character data for reports, keeps track of each number in a digital form, which is convenient when working in dollars and cents, and is relatively efficient in storage space. Most numeric data should be COMP-3.

Numeric Data Problems

Conversion   When numeric data of different types participate in an arithmetic operation, the compiler must convert the numbers to a common type for the operation. The conversion may take longer than the arithmetic operation. Minimize the conversions by using COMP-3 data. If the same DISPLAY item is to participate in an arithmetic operation several times, first move it to a COMP-3 data item to do the conversion only once.

Rounding   COBOL normally truncates the final results in arithmetic statements if their precision is greater than that of the identifier to which they are assigned. A result of 16.8 is truncated to 16 and a −4.1 is truncated to −4 if the resulting identifier has a precision of PIC S999. COBOL provides the ROUNDED phrase to round the final results rather than truncating them. A 16.8 would be rounded to 17 and a −4.1 rounded to −4. COBOL rounds a value whose rightmost digit is 5 up in absolute magnitude so that 4.5 is rounded to 5 and −4.5 is rounded to −5.

Rounding increases the accuracy, especially in repetitive operations. If we have records containing dollars and cents, which are summed and printed in units of whole dollars, a common error is to sum the numbers after rounding or truncating them. This is shown in the following columns of the report:

Full Accuracy	Rounded	Truncated
10.00	10	10
10.50	11	10
10.60	11	10
10.10	10	10
10.60	11	10
Total 51.80	53	50

Summing the rounded or truncated numbers gives a wrong total, even though it appears correct in that the individual numbers do sum to the total. The correct total is 51.80: 52 if rounded or 51 if truncated. When many numbers are summed, the results can be off considerably. Always compute the sum with the full precision and then round or truncate this sum as shown in the following columns:

Full Accuracy	Rounded	Truncated
10.00	10	10
10.50	11	10
10.60	11	10
10.10	10	10
10.60	11	10
Total 51.80	52	51

This gives the correct totals. Unfortunately they appear wrong because the individual numbers in the columns do not sum to the total, and there is always the person who checks computer reports with a hand calculator. Reports lose their credibility when you cannot add a column and obtain the total printed by the computer. Although the choice between correct totals that appear wrong and incorrect totals that appear correct is not a happy one, you should print the correct totals, even at the cost of appearing wrong. This particular problem could be avoided by printing the dollars and cents, even though the cents might not be of interest. Avoid either truncating or rounding whenever possible.

Intermediate Results   A major source of error is the intermediate results in arithmetic operations. If you saw the COBOL statement, COMPUTE $A = 6 * (2 / 4)$, would you expect it to yield a result of zero? It does because COBOL uses the precision of the data items in the arithmetic expression to determine the precision of the intermediate results. The (2 / 4) yields 0.5, but the precision of the intermediate result, determined by the 2 and 4, is PIC S9, and the 0.5 is truncated to zero. Zero times 6 yields zero.

The following precisions of intermediate results are for IBM System/370 computers. The precision is given by iVd, where i is the number of decimal digits to the left of the decimal point and d the number to the right.

Add, Subtract:

$i_1Vd_1 + i_2Vd_2$ yields $[1 + max(i_1, i_2)]V[max(d_1, d_2)]$

99V9 + 9V999 yields precision of 9(3)V9(3)

99.9   + 9.999 equals 109.899

Multiply:

$i_1Vd_1 * i_2Vd_2$ yields $(i_1 + i_2)V(d_1 + d_2)$

99V9 * 9V999 yields precision of 9(3)V9(4)

99.9 * 9.999 equals 998.9001

Divide:

i_1Vd_1 / i_2Vd_2 yields $(i_1 + d_2)V[max(d)]$

max(d) is the maximum of (d_1, d_2), or the d of the data item into which the result is stored

99V9 / 9V999, final result of 99V9 yields precision of 9(5)V9(3)

99.9 / 0.001 equals 99900.000

99V9 / 9V999, final result of 99V9(4) yields precision of 9(5)V9(4)

00.1 / 3.000 equals 00000.0333

Exponential:

If the exponent is a data item or noninteger literal:

  $i_1Vd_1 ** i_2Vd_2$ yields $[(i_1 * n) + (n - 1)]V[max(d)]$

max(d) is the maximum of (d_1, d_2), or the d of the final result field

n is the largest integer that i_1 permits

99V9 ** 9V, final result of 99V yields precision of 9(26)V

99V9 ** 9V, final result of 99V999 yields precision of 9(26)V999

If the exponent is an integer literal n:

  $i_1Vd_1 ** n$ yields $[(i_1 * n) + (n - 1)]V(d_1 * n)$

99V9 ** 2 yields precision of 9(5)V99

25.3 ** 2 equals 00640.09

Addition and subtraction generally cause no problems with intermediate results. Multiplication does if the result exceeds the total number of digits of precision allowed by the compiler, unlikely in commercial applications. Division causes the most problems. The result can exceed the total number of digits of precision when large numbers are divided by small ones. A more likely error is loss in precision caused by a division resulting in a fraction. We have seen how 6 * (2 / 4) yields zero. We could obtain the correct result by any of the following:

- Coding 6 * (2 / 4.0) to force the intermediate result to be carried to one decimal place.
- Defining the final result to have a decimal precision of V9 to force the intermediate result to be carried to one decimal place.
- Coding (6 * 2) / 4 to perform the division last. This method is preferable unless the result of the multiplication could exceed the maximum number of digits of precision. It works equally well for (6 * 1) / 3, whereas the two previous methods would give a result of 1.8.

All of this should be enough to convince you to check all calculations carefully for loss of intermediate precision.

Allocating Costs   Business applications often involve cost allocation of an amount or a pool proportionally across some base. A common example is allocating the overhead, where the total indirect charges for a department (the pool) might be allocated in proportion to the sales of each product. The usual calculation is

$$\text{amount allocated to item} = \frac{(\text{total amount to allocate}) \times (\text{sales of item})}{\text{total sales of all items}}$$

Obviously you should check the intermediate results closely when allocating costs. Because costs can only be allocated to the nearest cent, the sum of the calculated allocations often does not equal the exact amount to be allocated. This is shown in the following example:

Total amount to allocate = $1.00
Item A sales $2.22
Item B sales   3.33
Item C sales   <u>4.44</u>
   Total sales $9.99
Amount allocated to item A = 1.00(2.22/9.99) = $0.22
Amount allocated to item B = 1.00(3.33/9.99) =   0.33
Amount allocated to item C = 1.00(4.44/9.99) = <u>0.44</u>
   Total allocated   = $0.99

The total is off by 1¢. However, accountants get worried when things do not balance to the penny, and in many situations the amount can be large. This "float" is also an invitation to wrongdoing, and there is always a chance that it will simply disappear into someone's pocket. If the float cannot be eliminated, establish an account to contain it and create a transaction to credit or debit that account with the amount of the float. Then let the accountants worry about what to do with the amount.

Two passes through a file are often needed to do the allocation. The first pass computes the total pool amount, and the second pass allocates the pool to the individual base items. Alternatively, you may be able to sort the pool transactions to the front of the base transactions in the file so that you can read them first to compute the total pool amount before reading the individual base items and performing the allocation. This allows the allocation to be done in a single pass.

FLEXIBILITY THROUGH DATA

The degree of flexibility in a program depends to a large extent on the way the data is defined. Any unnecessary limitations on the data limit the program's flexibility. Consider the following guidelines in determining which form of data to use within a program.

- Enter and carry the minimum data necessary. For example, do not build attributes into a coding scheme, such as reserving a range of account numbers for overhead costs. Keep the account numbers in a table with an attribute indicating direct or overhead. Then you can change an account from direct to overhead with a simple table change.

- Use alphanumeric data unless arithmetic operations are performed. For example, a code might contain only the digits 1 to 9 to denote employee locations. Since arithmetic operations will not be performed on the field, make it alphanumeric. Then when a new location is added, as it surely will be, the location can be assigned values A, B, and so on, without having to enlarge the field.

- Have each data item serve a single function. To save space, a programmer will sometimes redefine the same area in a file to serve multiple purposes. This can be a bad practice. For example, the same area in a record might be used to record the date of the last salary increase and the date of termination. If an employee is rehired, you may need both dates for the calculation of the retirement benefits.

  Similar to this, a flag is sometimes used for several purposes. If you use the same flag for one purpose in one part of a program and for another somewhere else in the program, confusion results because a reader will not be sure which usage the program is testing. Have each flag serve a single purpose. If the program is so tight for storage that you cannot spend an extra byte for a flag, forget the program. It will be a disaster.

Elements in a table are often made to serve multiple functions, another bad practice. For example, a single field might denote both sex (male and female) and marital status (married or not) to save space. Four codes will cover all the possible combinations. The problem is that sex is separate from marital status, and it makes the field difficult to understand, complicates the programming, and gets complicated when other types of marital status are defined, such as divorced, widowed, and living together as close and dear friends.

- Allow room for growth. For data items with magnitudes that can increase, allow extra digits for growth. Remember the problems with gasoline pumps when the price of gasoline went over $1.00 a gallon. As a rule of thumb, use the maximum digits you think are reasonable, add one digit, think about inflation for a few minutes, and then add another digit.

- Carry the lowest level of detail, but eliminate unnecessary information. Once detail is lost in a file, it cannot be regained; but with detail you can always summarize. For example, do not carry the age of a person in a file, but only the birth date. The age can be computed from the birth date, but not the reverse. Also the age requires updating, but not the birth date.

- Do not take shortcuts with data. An example best illustrates this. A billing system was designed for a cable TV company to send notices to delinquent accounts. The programmer decided that rather than record the date for each amount owed, only the number of billings outstanding would be needed. The reasoning was that if three separate charges were outstanding, one would be for the current month and the other two would be for the two preceding months. Thus without reference to any dates, the program could make the assumption that the account was two months in arrears.

Now it gets sad. In one month a customer happened to order an accessory to connect a video tape recorder, added another outlet, and also ordered the movie selection box. The program treated these as three separate charges and assumed that the customer was three months in arrears. And so the customer received the standard nasty letter, saying something to the effect that unless he paid immediately, the company would come out and pillage and plunder until he did. It was a clever programming idea, but like most clever programming ideas, it failed.

TYPES OF DATA IN TRANSACTIONS

Now we turn to several forms of data common to business applications and to the operations performed on them.

Dates

Several dates are often carried in a transaction: the date the transaction originated, the date of booking (the effective date of the accounting transaction), the date of entry (when it is entered into the computer), and the date of processing. These dates are important for the audit trail and for validation and program logic. For example, the booking date can be compared to the accounting period end date to ensure that current transactions are being processed.

There are two common forms of dates, calendar and Julian. Calendar dates are of the form mm/dd/yy, although you must be aware of the European convention of writing the date as dd/mm/yy. Julian dates are of the form yy.ddd, where ddd is the sequential day of the year, between 1 and 366. The advantage of the Julian date is that it is easier to compute the number of days between two dates. The disadvantage is that people are more familiar with calendar dates. Dates are usually carried in numeric form (DISPLAY PIC 99 in COBOL) because arithmetic operations are performed on them.

For sorting it is easier if the date is carried in the file as yymmdd or yyddd. The sort can then treat the date as a single field. Two digits for the year may seem adequate, but many systems written today will still be running at the turn of the century. Then the sort on date is going to cause severe problems because a two-digit year will go from 99 to 00. Not much would be lost by carrying the year as four digits.

Computing a Leap Year   You often need to examine a date to determine whether it is a leap year in order to compensate for the extra day in February. Leap years are evenly divisible by 4. Divide the year by 4, and if there is no remainder, it is a leap year. This is shown in the following COBOL statements:

```
DIVIDE year BY 4 GIVING TALLY REMAINDER leap-year.
IF leap-year = ZERO
    THEN it-is-leap-year.
```

Computing Age   Another common operation is to compute an age in years given a birth date (*yymmdd*) and the current date (YYMMDD). In COBOL this could be done as:

```
IF MMDD NOT < mmdd
    THEN COMPUTE AGE = YY − yy
    ELSE  COMPUTE AGE = YY − yy − 1.
```

Converting Julian Date to Calendar Date   To convert a Julian date to a calendar date (or a calendar date to a Julian date) we need a table containing the days in each month:

```
01  CALENDAR.
      05   DAYS-IN-MONTH.
           10   JANUARY        PIC S99 COMP-3 VALUE 31.
           10   FEBRUARY       PIC S99 COMP-3.
*                 DAYS IN FEBRUARY CAN BE 28 OR 29.
           10   MARCH          PIC S99 COMP-3 VALUE 31.
                 .
                 .
                 .
           10   DECEMBER       PIC S99 COMP-3 VALUE 31.
      05   MONTH REDEFINES DAYS-IN-MONTH PIC S99 COMP-3
                 OCCURS 12 TIMES
                 INDEXED BY XMONTH.
```

To convert a Julian date YYDDD to a calendar date *yymmdd*, we begin by setting the index XMONTH to 1 to look at the first month in the table. If DDD is not greater than the days in the month, the table index XMONTH is the month (*mm*) and DDD is the day of the month (*dd*). If not, we subtract the days in that month from DDD and look at the next month in the table. The following COBOL statements do this:

```
                DIVIDE YY BY 4 GIVING TALLY REMAINDER leap-year.
                IF leap-year = ZERO
                    THEN MOVE 29 TO FEBRUARY
                    ELSE MOVE 28 TO FEBRUARY.
                MOVE DDD TO dd.
                PERFORM COMPUTE-JULIAN
                    VARYING XMONTH FROM 1 BY 1
                    UNTIL dd NOT > MONTH (XMONTH).
                SET mm TO XMONTH.
                MOVE YY TO yy.
****  DONE
           □    □
COMPUTE-JULIAN.
                COMPUTE dd = dd - MONTH (XMONTH).
****  EXIT
```

Converting Calendar Date to Julian Date   To convert a calendar date *yymmdd* to a Julian date YYDDD, we sum the days in the month table up to the current month and then add *dd:*

```
      MOVE ZEROS TO DDD.
      PERFORM SUM-DAYS
         VARYING XMONTH FROM 1 BY 1
         UNTIL XMONTH = mm.
      ADD dd TO DDD.
      MOVE yy TO YY.
****  DONE
            □   □
SUM-DAYS.
      ADD MONTH (XMONTH) TO DDD.
****  EXIT
```

Compute Days Between Two Dates The following COBOL statements illustrate a method of computing the number of days between two Julian dates, YY.DDD and *yy.ddd*, where YY.DDD is the most recent date:

```
      IF  YY = yy
         THEN COMPUTE days = DDD − ddd
         ELSE MOVE yy TO year
              PERFORM ADD-DAYS-IN-YEAR UNTIL year = YY
              ADD DDD TO days.
****  DONE
            □   □
ADD-DAYS-IN-YEAR.
      DIVIDE year BY 4 GIVING TALLY REMAINDER leap-year.
      IF leap-year = ZERO
         THEN MOVE 366 TO days-in-year
         ELSE MOVE 365 TO days-in-year.
      IF year = yy
         THEN COMPUTE days = days-in-year + 1 − ddd
         ELSE COMPUTE days = days + days-in-year
      ADD 1 TO year.
****  EXIT
```

To compute the days between two calendar dates, convert them to Julian dates and use this same method.

Calendars Contained in Tables If a program must calculate the number of working or business days between two dates, some form of calendar needs to be stored in the program as a table. A calendar is also needed in many systems to calculate the cumulative working days in a year or a quarter. If you were computing the daily interest on a savings account, but excluding weekends and holidays, you might use a calendar such as the following:

```
01  CY-CALENDAR.
*        DAILY CALENDAR FOR CALENDAR YEAR.
    05   CY-DAY OCCURS 366 TIMES INDEXED BY ICX
                  ASCENDING KEY IS CY-CALENDAR-DATE.
*        366 DAYS IN YEAR. A BINARY SEARCH WILL BE USED
*        FOR THE TABLE.
        10  CY-CALENDAR-DATE.
                CALENDAR DATE OF DAY.
*            15  CY-DATE-YR              PIC S9(4).
             15  CY-DATE-MO              PIC S99.
             15  CY-DATE-DY              PIC S99.
        10  CY-JULIAN-DATE.
*                JULIAN DATE OF DAY.
             15  CY-JULIAN-YR            PIC S9(4).
             15  CY-JULIAN-DY            PIC S9(3).
        10  CY-CUM-WORK-DAYS            PIC S9(3).
*                CUMULATIVE WORK DAYS IN YEAR.
        10  CY-TYPE-OF-DAY             PIC X.
*                W — WORK DAY
*                E — WEEKEND DAY
*                H — HOLIDAY
        10  CY-BIWEEKLY-PERIOD-END     PIC X.
*                Y — YES, OTHERWISE BLANK.
        10  CY-ACCT-PERIOD-END         PIC X.
*                Y — YES, OTHERWISE BLANK.
        10  CY-QUARTER-END             PIC X.
*                1, 2, 3, 4 FOR QUARTER END; ELSE BLANK.
        10  CY-YEAR-END                PIC X.
*                Y — YES, OTHERWISE BLANK.
```

The table could be initialized by reading the data into it so that the calendar can be changed each year. A date can be found in the table using a binary search:

```
SEARCH ALL CY-DAY
    AT END date-not-found
    WHEN CY-CALENDAR-DATE (ICX) = date
            table-entry-found.
```

Accounting Period

The solar system has not been kind to the accountant. The fact that the measurement of a day, one spin of the earth, is unrelated to the measurement of the year, the passage of the earth around the sun, results in a calendar not at all amenable to the cold logic of the computer.

The 365 or 366 days in a year are also unfortunate numbers because they are not evenly divisible into anything useful. The month, which is based upon the movement of the moon, works well as an accounting period because there are exactly 12 months in a year, and 12 is evenly divisible by 2 or 4 for semiannual or quarterly aggregations. However, the next division, the week, is unrelated to the month. Now it gets confusing.

Unless the company can convince its employees to live on a single paycheck a month, a semimonthly, biweekly, or weekly pay period is selected. If semimonthly, the end of a pay period falls on arbitrary days of the week, which makes scheduling a nightmare. If based on the week, the pay periods fall arbitrarily within the month, and not all months will contain the same number of pay periods. Since this distorts accounting reports, a four week accounting period is often used with a weekly or biweekly payroll.

But now the accounting periods do not exactly fit a year. If a company has a biweekly payroll and a four week accounting period, the 13 accounting periods in a year contain only 364 days. Furthermore, the 13 accounting periods do not divide evenly for semiannual or quarterly reporting. The usual solution is to establish something like 4, 3, 3, 3 accounting periods per quarter, and to not worry that one quarter is longer than the others and that the two semiannual periods are unequal.

When data is not summarized, the accounting period is not particularly troublesome. To report for an accounting period, a quarter, or semiannually, you need only select the detailed transactions that fall within these periods, whatever they happen to be.

When data is summarized, the problem becomes acute. If a report is to show year-to-date, quarter-to-date, and current period amounts, a file may have to be designed to contain the information, and the relationship between the pay period, accounting period, quarter, and year may dictate the layout of the record.

Data, especially management data, is usually more meaningful when compared with other data. Current period sales, for example, have more meaning when compared to the sales of the past three periods or of the same period last year. This is especially true in spotting trends and in analyzing the effect of management decisions.

Aside from the problems of gathering and storing the data, there is a problem in comparing periods that differ in length. If there are 20 days in the current period and only 18 days in the previous period because of holidays, the direct comparison is distorted. One solution is to put both periods on the same time basis. You might divide the amounts by 20 and 18, respectively, to put them on a daily basis, or convert the 18 day period to a 20 day period by multiplying its amount by $\frac{20}{18}$.

Another problem in comparisons with historic data is that almost anything can change in the interim. Account, job, and department numbers are the most likely to change. The data may not be available at the same level of detail. This is a price that a company pays for changing its accounts and its organization.

If the historical data is more detailed than the current data, you can aggregate it by using a table that maps the old data to the new data. If three accounts in the last year's data become a single account in this year's data, you can convert the three accounts of last year into this year's account with a table lookup. But if it goes the other way so that the current data is more detailed than the historical data, you may be stuck. If one account last year becomes three accounts this year, you may be able to allocate a fixed percentage to each, you may be able to allocate all of last year's account to one of this year's accounts, or you may have to do the allocation manually.

Percentages

Percentages must be converted into fractions by dividing them by 100 before use. That is, 50% of 10 is computed as $10 \times (50/100)$. Usually a percentage is converted to a fraction as soon as it is read in from a transaction, and it is carried internally as a fraction. Take care that you comment in the file whether the item is a percentage or a fraction. A percentage entered as PIC 999V9 would be carried internally as 9V999 in fractional form. COMP-3 is the best data type for fractions.

Organization

A transaction usually applies to a specific unit within an organization. In a cost system, an employee belongs to some department and does work for some department. Usually they are the same department, but not always. Consequently there is sometimes a need to record two organizations for cost transactions, the organization supplying the cost item and the organization to be charged with the cost. The organization is hierarchical. It should also be alphanumeric.

Account Number

All companies have a chart of accounts, and most transactions have an associated general ledger account number. The account is usually hierarchical. The account also has attributes, such as direct and indirect, asset and liability, and expense and revenue. Make the account number an alphanumeric data item.

Cost Object

The cost object tells what the cost was spent on, such as salary, material, or travel. Cost object is not a general term, but is defined here as a concept because it is so often needed in management reports. The cost object can be an aggregate of general ledger accounts. However, general ledger accounts are established by accountants for accounting purposes, and they may not provide the type of information required by operating managers, supervisors, and project leaders. Account numbers are usually too detailed for management reports.

The chart of accounts, for example, may contain an account for exempt and nonexempt salaries, because this information is needed for tax computations. But a manager may want to see salaries broken into sales, production, and maintenance rather than the categories of exempt and nonexempt. Consequently the cost object is often based on other than the general ledger account, such as function, location, or job title. The cost object is in effect the manager's equivalent of the account number. Like the account, it too has attributes, such as direct and indirect. Make the cost object an alphanumeric data item.

Job Number

The job number tells to what the cost is to be charged, and should be an alphanumeric data item. Most organizations have some form of job costing system. The job number collects costs for projects, locations, and activities. The job number is often hierarchical. In a project oriented system this would allow a contract to be broken up into workorders, projects, and tasks for costing, and then the costs could be aggregated to various levels for reporting.

Dollar Amount

Always carry dollar amounts in dollars and cents, even if only whole dollars are to be reported. You may need the cents for accuracy in forming totals, or a new report may require showing dollars and cents. Use COMP-3 for all dollar amounts.

Often debits and credits are carried as separate fields in records in order to balance the debits and credits. Even when debits and credits are carried separately, make the dollar amounts signed.

Hours

The conventional measurement of time in hours and minutes is inconvenient for use as data in the computer. Instead, time is usually carried in hours and fractions of hours as a COMP-3 data item. The minimum measurement of time in most situations is the minute, and two decimal places is sufficient for this. Always carry fractional hours to two decimal places so that there is the capability of being accurate to the minute.

If you must record the time of day, it is better to convert the time to the military convention of a 24 hour day for storage to avoid carrying A.M. and P.M. This also makes it easier to compute an elapsed time by subtracting the starting time from the ending time, being careful to account for the start of a new day.

IF start-time > end-time
   THEN elapsed-time = end-time + 24 − start-time
   ELSE elapsed-time = end-time − start-time.

When time is entered by hand, there is the question of whether to enter it in hours and minutes and convert it to fractional form inside the computer, or to enter time on the source input in fractional form. Should a person fill in 8 hours, 15 minutes, or 8.25 hours on a time sheet? Ultimately it does not matter all that much because people can adapt to either.

Descriptions

An extremely important but often ignored item of information to include in a source transaction is a description or comments field. The description field allows the user to comment the transaction. For correcting entries especially, the description may later prove valuable as part of the audit trail. The description field must be alphanumeric. Try to allow at least 25 characters.

Names

A person's name is composed of three parts, a first name, a middle name (or just the initial), and a last name. (In other countries people can have several more names, which make each person a walking genealogical chart.) The name fields should be alphanumeric. The following field sizes for names are suggested:

Last name   18 characters. According to the Guiness Book of Records, Featherstonehaugh, 17 characters, is the longest English name. Allow 18 to accommodate a new Guiness record.

First name   12 characters. Christabelle is the longest of the common given names.

Middle name 18 characters. The middle name is often a family name.

In addition to the name, there may be titles: Mr., Mrs., Ms. General, and The Right Honorable are prefixes; Jr. and Esq. are frequent suffixes. Allow room for them if necessary.

Since the name will probably be used in a sort and be printed, you must decide whether to carry it twice, or to carry the name once for the sort and write a program to format it for printing. Unless you have a yearning for an ulcer, carry the name twice in the file.

Addresses

An address is usually composed of the following:

Person's name (optional)
Company name (optional)
Division name (optional)
Street address and room, suite, or apartment number
City, state, zip code
Country (optional)

If you plan to sort on the city or state, you need to decide whether to carry them twice in the file, or to carry them once for the sort and write a program to format them for printing. The following field sizes are suggested:

Company name	50 characters. However, this will require abbreviating The Bank of America National Trust & Savings Association. International Minerals & Chemical is the longest of the Fortune 500 names.
Division name	50 characters. Same as for the company name.
Street address	40 characters. I doubt that many streets have longer names than my own—Mandeville Canyon Road—but allow some extra spaces for the street number and room, suite, or apartment number.
City	23 characters. If you can contain Southampton Long Island, other names should fit, too.
State	14 characters if spelled out. This accommodates the Carolinas. Allow 2 characters if the Post Office codes for the states are used.
Zip code	9 characters. (Going up from 5. Canada currently has 6 characters in its zip codes.)

Country

18 characters. Dominican Republic is the longest name not usually abbreviated. Allow 26 characters if you want to include The People's Republic of China, 37 characters if the Democratic People's Republic of Yemen (and Korea) is on your mailing list, and 38 characters for the longest name of a member of the UN: Byelorussian Soviet Socialist Republic.

THREE

Transactions in Business Applications

The heart of most business systems is the transaction. A transaction is a discrete event, such as a debit or a credit to an account, the addition of a record to a personnel file, or the updating of a payroll record with the current earnings. Transactions can originate from people, either by filling out input forms or by entering them from a terminal, or they can be generated by a computer. This chapter discusses the considerations necessary in designing and handling transactions.

AUDIT TRAIL

The audit trail is an important concept in the design of any business system because it provides documentary evidence that enables us to trace data in a system back to its origin. Thus the data in any report is traceable to some source document. The audit trail also works forward, enabling us to trace any transaction from its origin through the system. Aside from being required in accounting, the audit trail is an important debugging tool.

The audit trail may consist of a listing of source transactions, a report of totals by selected categories, and a new report of these totals when the transactions are summarized.

Fortunately computer data is rather stable. It does not grow, evaporate, or decay when stored. Consequently the audit trail is maintained by listings or summaries of the data going into a computer program, perhaps a listing of what the program is doing to the data, and reports or summaries of the data as it leaves the program. Source transactions should be listed in their original form. Totals may be generated on selected categories to enable data to be controlled when it is summarized. That is, if a program reads 10,000 transactions, summarizes them, and writes out 100 transactions, the total amount of some field in the 10,000 transactions should equal the total amount of the same field in the 100 transactions.

In order to provide an audit trail, you need to ask two related questions about any program being written. First, is there documentary evidence to enable someone to tell what went into the program and reconcile this with what came out of the program? Second, will this documentary evidence enable someone to trace the output of the program back to the data that entered the program?

As an example of an audit trail, suppose that you lived in a checkless society in which you received your entire pay each week in cash. Now suppose that each payday you hand a wad of bills to an old drinking buddy to take on down to the IRS for your withholdings. An audit trail must tell you whether the amount you gave your friend is the amount that reached the IRS. (If not, you will have to lean on your friend.) The audit trail must also tell the IRS whether the amount they received is the amount you sent. (If not, the difference becomes income to your friend upon which the IRS will expect to collect tax.) The audit trail ensures accuracy and establishes credibility.

THE FUNCTION OF TRANSACTIONS

Transactions have two broad functions. They can be cumulative—they are merely added to a file; or they can be updating—they change records in a file. The system flow chart in Figure 2 illustrates the difference.

Cumulative Transactions

Many accounting transactions are cumulative. For example, a cost ledger file could be generated by merging all the current period transactions. These transactions could then be merged with transactions from previous periods to generate quarterly, semiannual, and annual reports. Cumulative transactions are easy to handle because the logic of adding transactions to a file is simple. Complications come in later when the data is summarized for reporting or retention.

Cumulative transactions are usually stored in sequential files. Since the transactions are not associated with any existing records in the file, they need not be uniquely identifiable. Duplicate records in the file may be perfectly acceptable.

Updating Transactions

Updating transactions update the records in a file. There are four actions that the updating transaction can perform. The transaction can be added to the file as a new record, the transaction can update or change values in

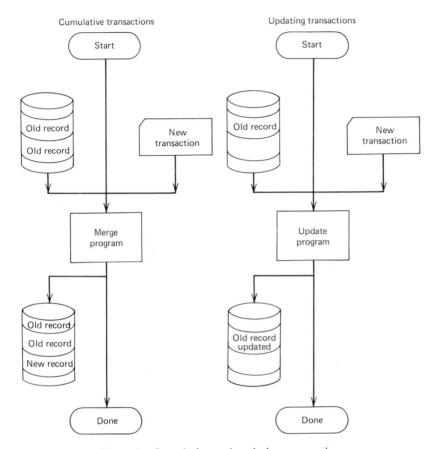

Figure 2 Cumulative and updating transactions.

an existing record in the file, the transaction can replace an existing record in the file, and the transaction can delete an existing record in the file. (Some systems have only three actions, where the replace is accomplished by a delete and an add.) For example, a personnel system would have new employees added when they are hired, existing records would be updated as personnel information changes, and the records would be eventually deleted for terminated employees.

For updating transactions, each transaction must have a unique identifier or record key which is used to identify the record in the file being updated. There cannot be more than one record in the file having the same key, or the transaction will have no way of knowing which record to update. Updating transactions are used with both sequential and direct-access files.

There are times when you want a single transaction to update several records. This complicates the updating. One way to do this is to allocate two keys to the transaction, a start and an end range, rather than a single key. Then all the records that lie within this range are updated. The second way is to use a generic key in the transaction. For example, the record keys might be eight characters. If you specify only "ABC" as the transaction key, the transaction would update all records containing "ABC" as the first three characters of their eight character record keys. Fortunately, such applications are rare.

DATA IN TRANSACTIONS

Common Data

Some attributes common to most transactions should be carried as data in the transaction itself.

Transaction Type   You should uniquely identify each type of transaction in a system by carrying the type as an alphanumeric data field in the transaction itself. This enables a program to check that it is receiving only the proper types of transactions. In one dishonorable system the program did not check for transaction type, and an operator error allowed a tape label to be processed as a transaction. Some very strange reports were generated before the problem was discovered.

Origin   Carry the origin in the transaction as an alphanumeric field. The origin can be a person's ID and terminal number for an on-line terminal, or a form, page, and line number from an input form. This information forms part of the audit trail.

Updating   For updating transactions, an action field is necessary to indicate whether to add a transaction to the file, to delete a record, to replace a record, or to update a record with values from the transaction. A convenient way to do this is to use a one character alphanumeric field with an 'A' denoting addition, 'D' deletion, 'C' a change, and 'R' replace. In a sort, these four codes fall into the following order when multiple transactions with the same key occur within a single update run:

A	Add the transaction.
C	Change the record.
D	Delete the record.
R	Replace the record.

If you do not allow multiple transactions with the same record key in a run, the sort order of the action field does not matter. If you do want multiple transactions in the same run as for a weekly run in which a Monday transaction might add a record and a Friday transaction might change it, the sort order of the action field is important. Rather than the add, change, delete, and replace order, the delete should either come last (to apply all transactions to a record before deleting it), or first (to effect a replace by deleting and then adding a record). So a different mnemonic might be used for the action field to replace the transactions in the desired sort order as follows:

D   Delete the record.

I   Insert the transaction (a synonym for add).

M   Modify a record (a synonym for change).

R   Replace a record.

Date   Some date, whether it is the booking date, the date the transaction was submitted, the date processed, or all of these, ought to be in the transaction. Usually the booking date is included, with the date submitted being placed on the batch of transactions and the date processed on a header record in a transactions file.

Error Override Flag   Validation of input data will encounter situations in which the data appears bad to the validation program, but is in fact good. An error override flag may be needed to tell the system to process the transaction even though the data falls outside the expected limits.

Record Key   If the transaction is updating a file, there must be some way to associate the transaction with the corresponding record in the file. For a sequential update, the file and the transactions must be in sort order based upon this record key. For direct-access files, the record keys do not need to be in sort order. In planning a system, the items that will uniquely identify each record must be thought out and included in each transaction that updates the file.

Sources of Data

Data in a transaction can originate from the source transaction, it can be computed from data in the transaction, or it can be looked up in a table or file. For example, an employee's department can be coded on timekeeping sheets, or it can be obtained from the payroll file using the employee ID to access the file. In a sales transaction, the total sales amount could be computed from the unit price and the quantity sold.

Filling out input forms is simplified, and a possible source of input error is eliminated when information is looked up in a table or file. However, there may be instances where the value carried in the table or file must be overridden, as when an adjustment to a prior period is made for a time when the employee was in another department. A simple way of handling these situations is to enter the item only when it is to override a value in a table or file.

Looking up values from a file becomes more complicated when the field in the transaction is not in sort order. The file used for the lookup may have to be direct access. If transactions updating a personnel file are in employee ID order and the department number in the same transaction is to be validated in a file, the department numbers in the transactions will be in essentially random order, precluding the use of a sequential lookup in the file. For efficient searching, the file either must be read into a table or made direct access.

Another way to simplify input and reduce error is the turnaround document. A turnaround document is generated by the computer and contains information obtained from files. People filling out the form can correct or override the preprinted information, in addition to filling out the remainder of the form. The document is then entered as a transaction. Time sheets are often made turnaround documents in which the employee's ID, name, department, and perhaps even personnel information are printed on the time sheet. The employee fills in the hours and may make change to the other information as necessary.

SUMMARIZATION

Summarization is done to reduce the amount of storage space required, to reduce processing time, and to simplify programming. For example, a general ledger report might contain a current-month and a year-to-date amount. If the file were in detail form, containing each individual transaction affecting an account, this would result in processing a large number of transactions at year-end. The following example illustrates such transactions:

Individual transactions:

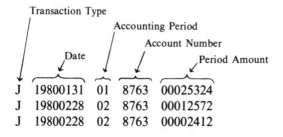

Transaction Type	Date	Accounting Period	Account Number	Period Amount
J	19800131	01	8763	00025324
J	19800228	02	8763	00012572
J	19800228	02	8763	00002412

We might summarize by account number by period so that there is a single transaction for each account for each accounting period, greatly reducing the transaction volume if there were many transactions:

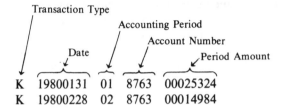

```
K   19800131   01   8763   00025324
K   19800228   02   8763   00014984
```

There are two ways to carry the data in a summarized file. One is to carry a single record for the full summarization level as just shown. The other method is to carry multiple fields within the record. In our example we might summarize by account and create a single record containing each period's amount. This would reduce the volume of transactions even further and simplify writing reports requiring year-to-date and current-period amounts. However, the summarized file must be updated each period.

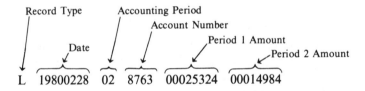

```
L   19800228   02   8763   00025324   00014984
```

Historical data may also be a candidate for summarization. Such data as sales and production figures have more meaning when compared to the previous period's figures or even the corresponding figures from the preceding year. If a report is to show quarterly amounts and a year-to-date amount, it could contain four fields, one for each quarter. The year-to-date amount would be the sum of the four.

Detail is lost at each level of summarization. A file in which a single record contains year-to-date and current-period amounts cannot be used for a report in which current-period and previous-period amounts are wanted. We would have to modify the file to add another field for the previous period.

In deciding between summarization and detail, the tradeoff is between processing efficiency and simplicity on the one hand and programming flexibility on the other. There is also some effort required to update the summarized file, and a reset program may be necessary. For example, the quarter-to-date field must be reset to zero at the end of each quarter. This might be done within the summarizing program by having it recognize the start of a new quarter.

Summarization is accomplished by deciding on the fields upon which to summarize, sorting on these fields, and then reading and summing all transactions in which the summation fields have the same values. Summarization often includes selection in some hierarchical order. As an example, suppose that we are told to prepare a summary file for a year-end sales report with a line for each person showing the sales for each month during the year. Furthermore, suppose that we are to include all sales transactions of $200 or more and to exclude all sales transactions from Hawaii.

The first step is to resolve the conflict in the inclusion and exclusion. Is a $200 sale in Hawaii to be included or excluded? Inclusion and exclusion logic is often full of ambiguity and must be nailed down. We will assume that a $200 sale in Hawaii is to be excluded. Notice also that implicit in the report is the summation hierarchy—by person and then by month.

For simplicity in reporting, we might summarize to create a single record for each person, with monthly sales contained within the record as a table. The steps to create this record would be as follows:

1   Exclude records for sales in Hawaii.
2   Include records with sales amounts of $200 or more.
3   Sort the selected records on person. The sort is done after the selection so that the excluded records are not sorted. Because we are storing the month's sales for each person in a table, we need not sort on month. If we were creating a separate record for each person for each month, we would then need to sort on month.
4   Initialize the output record and read the sorted records until a new person is encountered, summing the monthly sales amounts into the proper slot in the table. When a new person is encountered, write out the record, initialize the record areas, and proceed.

PROBLEMS WITH TRANSACTIONS

Individual Field Updating

Alphanumeric fields are always changed by replacement, but there are two ways to change numeric fields: by replacement or by arithmetic addition. If you are updating historical data with current transactions, you will want to add the data. If the data is not cumulative or is being corrected, you will want to replace rather than add. The type of transaction dictates what is needed. Seldom will you need both, but when you do, you can precede the updating field with a flag that tells whether to replace or to add:

```
IF flag = some-value
    THEN ADD trans-amount TO master-amount
    ELSE  MOVE trans-amount TO master-amount.
```

A transaction may have the potential of updating several fields in a record, but may be used to update only a single field. The simplest way to do this is to adopt the convention that fields are filled in only if they are to update the corresponding field in the record. This requires that all numeric fields be redefined as alphanumeric so that they can be tested for blanks.

For alphanumeric fields that are to be updated with blanks, adopt some convention to indicate blanks. Coding all asterisks (*) on the input form could mean that the field is to be set to blanks, assuming that you would never update a field with asterisks.

```
IF transaction-field = ALL "*"
    THEN MOVE SPACES TO record-field.
```

Fields are usually identified by their fixed position within the transaction. This is clumsy where a file contains a large number of fields but only a few are updated with each transaction. Rather than creating a very large transaction with fixed-position fields, we can assign an identifying number to each field in the record and include this field number in the transaction to indicate the field to update. If a record contained 500 fields, the field number (1 to 500) could be included on the transaction along with the field value, as shown in the following example.

Transaction with fixed-position fields:

Key	Field 1	Field 2	Field 3	· · ·	Field 500

Transaction with numbers identifying the fields:

Key	n	Field n value	n	Field n value	· · ·

If all the fields in the record have the same length, the record can be described as a table and the field number used as an index to store the transaction value in the record. If the field sizes differ, as they likely will, the field number can be used in a GO TO . . . DEPENDING ON sentence with separate COBOL statements to handle each field number. The following example illustrates this:

Transaction:

| T | XXXXXX | 012 | ALPHANUMERIC DATA ITEM |

| T | XXXXXX | 011 | 002265 |

The transaction record is first described:

```
01   TRANS-RECORD.
     05   TRANS-TYPE            PIC X.
     05   TRANS-KEY             PIC X(6).
     05   TRANS-FIELD.
          10   TRANS-FIELD-NO        PIC S9(3).
          10   TRANS-FIELD-ALPHA   PIC X(20).
          10   TRANS-FIELD-NUMERIC REDEFINES
                    TRANS-FIELD-ALPHA.
*              THE TRANSACTION FIELD CAN BE REDEFINED
*              TO CARRY THE NECESSARY VALUES.
               15   TRANS-FIELD-NUMBER   PIC S9(4)V9(2).
               15   FILLER                     PIC X(14).
```

The individual fields would be updated as follows when a transaction is read:

```
     GO TO FIELD-1,
             FIELD-2,

                .
                .
                .

             FIELD-n
     DEPENDING ON TRANS-FIELD-NO.
               □  □
FIELD-11.
     MOVE TRANS-FIELD-NUMBER TO field-11-in-record.
     GO TO done.
FIELD-12.
     MOVE TRANS-FIELD-ALPHA TO field-12-in-record.
     GO TO done.
```

Which Fields to Update

A problem in designing an updating transaction is to decide which fields can be changed. The solution is easy—allow any field to be changed. Even data that is "unchangeable" may have to be changed if it gets into the computer incorrectly, and almost anything can get into a computer incorrectly, no matter how hard you try to prevent it. Once there, you must correct it.

Updating the Record Key

If the records being updated are in sort order on the record key, you have a problem when you update the record key, because this puts the record out of sort sequence. In a random-access file you must delete the old record and write the new record into the file. In a sequential file you can sort the master file after updating; or, more efficiently, with a little more effort, you can write the records whose key is being changed into a separate file and then later sort and merge the new file with the master file. For this you might set a special job completion code when records are written into the file, and then invoke the merge as a separate job step only when the special completion code is set.

Audit Trail

As part of your audit trail, you need to indicate the updating done to the record. A simple way to do this is to print the record before it is updated, print the transactions updating it, and print the updated record. This lets you know exactly what has happened:

```
ORIGINAL:      L 19800228 02 8763 00025324 00014984
TRANSACTION:   T 19800228 02 8764
TRANSACTION:   T 19800228 02        00003311
UPDATED:       L 19800228 02 8764 00028635 00014984
```

You might also print asterisks under the fields that were changed. To reduce the amount printed, you might print the before and after of just the fields changed in the record.

Transaction Size

Transactions entered on cards and other fixed-length record forms may require multiple entries per transaction. A moderately complex personnel/payroll system may require 600 characters of input for a transaction to add a new employee. Using card input, this requires several input cards per transaction.

Multiple input records per transaction make the validation considerably more complex because we must ensure that all the required parts of a transaction are present, that there are no duplicate parts, and that they are in the proper sequence. The records composing a transaction must each be uniquely identified as being a part of the same transaction so that they can be sorted, and that we can detect if they are out of order. Multiple record transactions are usually reformatted and written out as a single record after validation.

Initialization

A record in a program that is used to create an output record must first be initialized, generally by moving spaces to the alphanumeric fields and zeros to the numeric fields. Suppose that the following record must be initialized:

```
01   A.
     05   B       PIC  X(10).
     05   C       PIC  S9(5) COMP-3.
     05   D       PIC  X(3).
     05   E       PIC  S9(5) COMP-3.
```

The record can be initialized by assigning initial values to the elementary items, but this initializes only the first record written, and all records should be initialized. The easiest way to initialize a record is to move SPACES to the record as a group item and then move ZEROS to the numeric items:

```
MOVE SPACES TO A.
MOVE ZEROS TO C,
              E.
```

If the record is to be initialized from several places within the program, the above could be made a paragraph and performed. Now suppose that the following record needs to be initialized:

```
01   RECORD-OUT.
     05   SCHOOL        PIC  X(25).
     05   CHILDREN      OCCURS 600 TIMES
                        INDEXED BY IX.
          10   AGES     PIC  S9(3) COMP-3.
```

The record contains a table of 600 elements. We can initialize the table in a loop, but doing this for each record is inefficient. A more efficient way to do this, at some cost in memory, is to define a new record that contains the same number of characters as the record to be written. By initializing the original record only once and moving it to the new record, we can initialize the output record whenever we wish by moving the new record to it. This works especially well when initial values are assigned to the first record, or when the initialization values are computed with the program. The following illustrates this technique:

```
01  ZERO-IT        PIC X(1225).
    □      □
    MOVE SPACES TO SCHOOL.
    PERFORM A20-PART-A
        VARYING IX FROM 1 BY 1
        UNTIL IX > 600.


    MOVE RECORD-OUT TO  ZERO-IT.
    □      □
A20-PART-A.
    MOVE ZERO TO AGES (IX).
```

[Same size as RECORD-OUT]

[This initializes the record; rather than doing this each time, we save a copy of the record after it has been initialized and simply move the copy to the record hereafter]

[Save initialized record]

Now whenever we wish to initialize RECORD-OUT, we do the following:

```
    MOVE ZERO-IT TO RECORD-OUT.
```

[Move initialized copy to the record]

FOUR

Validation

To a computer file, the world teems with potential hardware, software, and human errors, all engaged in a gigantic conspiracy to render its frail contents useless. The only thing standing between the file and this unspeakable fate is the validation, or editing, done on the input data. Bad data is like the plague to a medieval city. If it is not stopped before entering, it spreads its poison to everything it touches, soon infecting the entire population.

Hardware errors should be the least likely cause of problems because of the high reliability of computers and the redundancy and error correcting codes built into them. And when hardware errors do occur, lights flash, bells ring, and hoards of technicians descend on the computer with brief-cases stuffed with tools. The best errors are those that announce themselves with fanfare. The worst are those that give no indication that something has gone haywire.

Software errors, both in the operating system and in the application, program, will take their toll. They can also be subtle, giving no indication that something went wrong. In one system, under certain circumstances, the operating system would not write out the last block when a file was closed. For most runs there would be no problem, but every so often the last few records would not be written into the file. This type of error is dia-bolical because there is no indication that anything has gone wrong.

Human error will account for most problems in a production program. Its frequency is exceeded only by its ingenuity. Humans are at their most creative when they make errors. For validating manually prepared trans-actions, few assumptions can be made about the data. Numeric fields may not contain numeric data, and required fields may be missing. For such transactions the only safe assumptions within a program are those that would prohibit the program accessing the data: wrong record length or for-mat, wrong block size, or wrong file access method. Everything else is suspect.

SERIOUSNESS OF ERRORS

Errors vary in their seriousness, and this determines the action to be taken when they are discovered. There are four levels of seriousness: terminal, reject, warning, and note.

Terminal Errors

A terminal error is one that requires terminating a program. Processing a file with the wrong accounting date is such an error. There should be few errors of this type. For example, a person missing from the payroll file might be thought to be terminal, but it may be better to continue processing the payroll so that everyone else gets paid and write the check for the person by hand.

Errors in data should never be allowed to cause a program to abnormally terminate. Conditions that would cause abnormal termination, such as processing nonnumeric data when numeric data is expected, should be detected and handled by the program.

Reject Errors

A reject error is one in which a transaction must be corrected before it can be accepted. A person missing from the payroll file would be a reject error.

Warning Errors

A warning error is one in which the data appears wrong and is not accepted, but may actually be valid. A transaction debiting petty cash for $100,000 might actually be correct. There must be a means of overriding the warning if the transaction is later verified as correct.

Note Errors

A note error is one in which the data is accepted and an information message is printed. This is more of a "you told me to let you know when this happened" type of event than an error. An employee receiving more than four hours of overtime might merit a note.

ACTION TAKEN ON ERRORS

The action taken on errors depends on their seriousness, but ultimately it boils down to printing an error message and accepting or rejecting the transaction. However, nothing is ever this simple.

Rejecting Transactions

The variations in rejecting transactions are: (1) reject all transactions; (2) reject only the transaction in error; (3) accept the good in the transaction and reject the bad; (4) accept the transaction, changing bad values to some predetermined good values; or (5) accept the transaction and ignore the error.

Rejecting All Transactions   We may wish an error in any transaction to cause all transactions to be rejected, even those already validated. This is done if no data can be processed until all data is ready for processing. This also requires the validation to be done as a separate step before the updating. The bad transactions must be corrected and all transactions validated again. This continues until all transactions pass the validation.

Although this technique is simple, it can be expensive in processing time. The same result can be obtained by writing the good and the bad transactions into separate files, correcting the bad transactions, recycling them through the validation program, merging the newly validated transactions with the good transactions file, and continuing the process until all transactions are validated. The disadvantage is that it is more complicated to program. This technique is discussed in more detail later in this chapter.

Reject the Transaction in Error   If a transaction is not critical to a run, it can be rejected and resubmitted later. A change of the person to notify in case of accident in a personnel file might be such an example.

Accepting Part of a Transaction   If a transaction is updating a file, we can accept valid fields and reject the invalid ones. The problem with this technique is that it is difficult to recreate the portion of the transaction to be resubmitted, and it is easy to overlook fields that were in error.

Assuming Values for Invalid Fields   If a field is invalid, sometimes a value can be assumed for it so that it is accepted. If an accounting transaction has an invalid account, it might be assigned to a special holding account in order to get the transaction into the system. It can then be backed out from the account and resubmitted to the proper account later.

Accepting the Transaction   For warning and note errors the transaction can be accepted. The note errors would be automatically accepted, but some sort of error override flag may be needed for warning errors. This allows human intervention to examine the error and determine whether to allow the item to go through.

Error Messages

Every error should produce a message to do the following:

- Print the transaction involved.
- Tell the severity of the error (terminal, reject, warning, or note).
- Tell what the error is.
- Tell which field within the transaction is in error. One way to do this is to print asterisks or some other character under the invalid field.
- Explain what the program will do with the error. (Assume a value for the field, reject the transaction, or terminate the program.)
- Tell what, if anything, should be done outside the program. (Perhaps increase a table size and recompile.)

Example:

JOHN T. DOE   24.6   3345.7   13/01/1982
                          **

ERROR—BAD DATE, TRANSACTION REJECTED.

DETECTING ERRORS

There are four broad areas where data errors can occur: in a file, in a batch of transactions, in a single record or transaction, and in an individual field.

File Validation

Errors affecting a file are usually terminal, and processing should not continue. The operating system provides several ways to protect files, but other safeguards may also be programmed.

Volume Serial Number For tape volumes and mountable direct-access storage volumes, the operating system usually provides for volume serial number checking. Always use this to ensure that the proper volume is mounted. The system rejects a volume whose volume serial number (which is contained on the volume as data) does not match that supplied in the JCL.

Data Set Name The operating system usually has provision for storing the name of the data set (or file) in its label and checking that the name on the data set matches that supplied by the JCL. Always use standard labels and supply the data set name for additional safety.

Header Record   You can write the first record of a file as a header record in order to contain information that uniquely identifies the contents of the file. The header record ensures that the records are those wanted. The data might include the accounting periods covered, the period end date, and the type of records the file contains. Some operating systems provide facilities for nonstandard labels, but they are rather complicated. It is simpler to write the first record in the file as the header record, redefining it to contain a field that identifies it as the header record, the date, the accounting periods, and whatever else is needed to verify that the proper file is being processed.

Trailer Record   The trailer record is the last record written in the file. It could contain a record count and any hash totals of critical fields. (Hash totals are described later in this chapter.) The presence of the trailer record ensures that the last record intended was written, the record count ensures that all the records are present, and the hash totals ensure that values have not changed in the fields being checked.

Like the header record, the trailer record should be of the same length as the other records in the file, redefined to include a code that identifies it as a trailer record, the record count, and whatever hash totals are wanted. The following illustrates a file containing header and trailer records. Note that the first byte allows the header and trailer records to be sorted into the proper place.

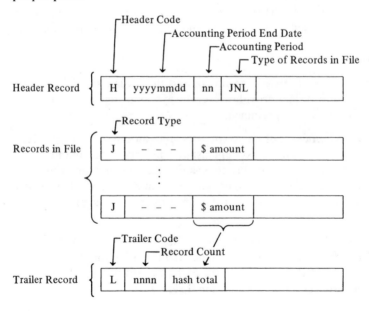

Some operating systems automatically write a trailer record that contains the number of records in the data set, and then compare this count with the records read when the file is closed after input. Use this facility when provided.

Batch Validation Batch totals ensure that data is not keyed incorrectly, misinterpreted, or lost from the time it leaves the originator until it is processed in the computer. With each group or batch of transactions, generally all those on an input form or group of input forms, critical numeric fields, usually dollar amounts, are totaled by hand. The batches are checked by instructing the computer to compute the batch total, which is then compared with the manual total. If a transaction is lost or keyed improperly, the error is detected. Individual batch totals can also be summed to obtain a grand total as a safeguard against losing an entire batch.

Checking batch totals can be done either manually or on the computer. When done manually, a person must compare the manual totals against the batch totals generated by the computer. Not only is this slow, it also uses people to poor advantage. Their ability to make input errors is perhaps exceeded by their ability to make errors in checking batch totals.

Alternatively, the batch totals and perhaps a transaction count can be entered with the transactions as data. This allows the computer to compare this total with the total computed from the individual transactions in the batch. Such drudgery is what computers do best.

The batch record is usually the first or last record in a batch. The transactions must be given a code to identify them as belonging to the same batch, and this batch code is carried with the transactions to provide an audit trail. The following example illustrates batch controls:

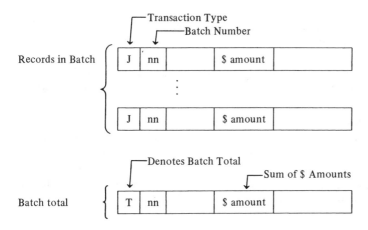

If transactions contain debits and credits that must balance to zero, this validation should be performed on the batches. When a batch error occurs, there is no way to tell which transaction in the batch is in error. Consequently the entire batch must be rejected.

Hash Totals   The batch total is not to check against the computer doing something wrong so much as to protect against human error. A hash total is the usual internal safeguard against the computer making an error or dropping a record or transaction. A hash total is created by summing a numeric field within a record while the file is being written, and then writing this total as the last record in the file. It is termed a hash total because the amount has no meaning. In fact, nonnumeric fields in some systems can also be summed by moving them to a PIC 999 . . . 9 field to strip off the zone bits and leave only numeric characters, which can be summed. Then when the file is read, the fields are again summed and checked against the total in the last record. If the totals do not match, either a record was lost or a field was changed.

Although it may seem paranoiac to go to this extreme to protect against hardware errors, sometimes paranoia is justified. However, the increasing reliability of computer hardware with the parity and error correcting codes has made hash totals less necessary.

Number of Transactions or Records   The number of transactions or records being processed may have allowable limits. Any transactions read into a table must not exceed the table size. It is also considerate to print a warning when a table is close to being filled. There may also be some minimum or maximum number of records or transactions that can be reasonably expected. Just printing the number of records read or written often gives enough information to tell that something went wrong.

File Dump   An often neglected tool in a system is a program or utility to dump a file. It is used to examine files for debugging. This program or utility should be written and maintained as part of the system. It helps to have a provision to begin dumping some number of records into the file, and to dump some specified number of records. The file dump may be formatted or unformatted. A formatted dump is easier to read, but there are times when an unformatted dump is necessary. For example, an alphanumeric field may print as blanks but actually contain nonblank but invalid characters. An unformatted dump would show the invalid characters.

An unformatted dump is usually provided as a standard utility program in most operating systems. The dump, in hexadecimal or character form, is difficult to read for packed-decimal or binary information. Some software products, such as DYL260, are available that combine the best of both. They are easy to code to print either a formatted or an unformatted dump, and have sophisticated record selection.

Record or Transaction Validation

Transaction Type All transactions ought to contain a transaction type to ensure that the proper transaction is being received.

Sequence If there is a sequence number associated with transactions, such as a line number on an input form, it can be checked to see if the transactions are in the proper order (if it matters), that no transactions are missing, and that there are no duplicate transactions.

When a single transaction consists of multiple physical records, the physical records should be checked for sequence. For example, a transacton requiring 170 characters entered on cards would require at least three cards per transaction. The cards should be sequenced and checked to ensure that they are in the proper order, that no cards are missing, and that there are no duplicate cards. The following example illustrates this:

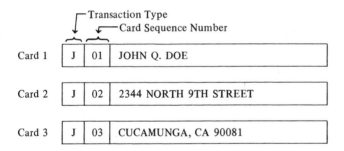

Record Key The data items within a record or transaction that uniquely identify it are termed the record key. Usually the record key must be validated. For updating transactions, such as a personnel file update where the transaction is being added, the record key (employee ID) must not match a record key already in the file. If the transaction is updating or deleting a record, a record that contains the same record key must be in the file. For cumulative transactions, such as an accounting transaction being merged with other transactions, the record key might be validated in a table or file.

The validation can be done with either direct or sequential access or with a table lookup. For sequential access, both the transactions being validated and the file being used for validation must be in the same sort order on the record key. With random access, the transactions need not be in sort order.

Sometimes an internal table can be used rather than direct access, which is more efficient because the I/O is greatly reduced. If the file being used for validation is not too large, define a table to contain only the record keys, read the file, and store the record keys in the table. If the file is in sort order, the more efficient binary search can be used.

Design the transactions so that they can be sorted into their proper order. With the disappearance of punched cards in favor of key to tape and disk devices, there is no longer the risk of dropping card decks, but transactions can still get out of order (by not being in the right order to begin with). Even if you do not sort the transactions, you need the facility to sort them because this same logic is necessary to check that they are in order.

In the cards containing names and addresses in the previous example, there was no means of sorting the records. If they got out of order, how could CUCAMUNGA, CA, be associated with JOHN Q. DOE? When there are several physical records per transaction, the records must contain something to identify them as belonging together. A record key consisting of the employee ID would accomplish this.

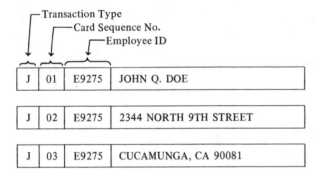

Printing Transactions   An audit trail is essential. The audit trail often consists of listings of all data read and written by the program. It may also consist of the files themselves if programs are available to print their contents. Alternatively we might print all the transactions read or written by the program if there are few, or print the transactions on request if there are many. The latter is handy for debugging, but less useful in production jobs, because once the program is run and an error discovered, it is too late to request an audit trail from the program unless it is rerun.

Programs should always print at least the following for the audit trail:

- Number of records read and written for each file.
- Number of records selected if there is selection logic.

- Any relevant totals, such as the total dollar amount of the transactions read or written.
- The progress of the program's execution through its major phases. At a minimum, print when the program begins and ends execution.

For a file being updated by transactions, print the updating transaction and the changed record before and after updating.

Field Validation

All the fields in manually prepared transactions should be validated. The fields of file records and computer-generated transactions require much less, if any, field validation.

Class Test   The class test checks that the data is of the proper type: numeric or alphabetic. Because nonnumeric data in a numeric field will abnormally terminate a program if arithmetic operations are performed on it, always use the class test on numeric fields.

Presence of Data   If a field is required, test for its presence. In transactions that update an existing file, it is a common practice to code only the fields to be changed, leaving the remaining fields blank. For a numeric field, re-define the field as alphanumeric to test for blanks. If it is blank, ignore it. If it is not blank, apply the class test.

Range Check   Numeric values are often tested for reasonable or permissible limits. Dates are checked to ensure that they are greater than the previous period end date and less than or equal to the current period end date. Alphanumeric fields, such as codes consisting of consecutive values, can also be checked for range. For numeric ranges, two limits may be checked: an absolute limit (serious error) and a reasonable limit (warning error). But usually one limit is enough.

Specific Values   Often codes must contain only specific values. For example, a field containing a person's sex could be checked for F or M and anything else rejected.

The value of some fields must often be validated in a table or even a file. For example, a time sheet transaction in which a person charges to an account would require the employee ID to be validated in the personnel file, and the account number also to be validated, perhaps in an account table or file.

Consistency   Consistency checks are done when the value of one field is related to the value of another. For example, a cost transaction containing an employee ID should have a value in the hours field. There may be a re-

quirement that only people belonging to specific departments be allowed
to charge to certain accounts.

Visual Proofing For many alphanumeric fields and some numeric fields,
nothing works as well as having a person read the transaction. One of the
things we humans do well, but which computers do poorly, is to glance at a
name and tell if it is correct.

Self-Checking Numbers Self-checking numbers derive from techniques in
which the digits in the numbers themselves are used to detect invalid codes.
This is usually done by appending a check digit calculated from the number. There are many techniques for calculating check digits, but the modulus 10 and modulus 11 methods are the most popular ones because hardware features are available on data entry devices to generate check digits.
To illustrate the modulus 10 method, we will generate a check digit for the
code 47268.

1 Starting with the right-most digit and working toward left, form a number from every other digit:

$$47268$$
$$428$$

2 Multiply this number times 2. ($2 \times 428 = 856$)
3 Sum the digits of this new number and the digits in the original number
   not multiplied by 2:

$$856 \quad 47268$$
$$8+5+6+7+6 = 32$$

4 Subtract this number from the next higher number ending in zero (40)
   to form the check digit:

$$40 - 32 = 8$$

   If the sum had ended in 0, say 30, the difference would be 10, in which
   case 0 is used for the check digit.
5 Append the check digit to the code to form the self-checking number:
   472688

   If two digits are transposed, such as 427688, the check digit calculated
from this is 2, which does not match the 8. Check digits are best at catching
transpositions and incorrect keying of a digit.

Self-checking numbers are used for preassigned codes, such as employee numbers or credit card numbers. The self-checking number can tell if a code is invalid, but it cannot tell for certain that the code is valid. Self-checking numbers are best used for screening where there is no easy access to a list of valid codes.

CORRECTING ERRORS

After the transactions have been validated, some of them will be found to contain errors that need correcting. They may either be corrected before the system is run, or corrected and submitted later. In either event you must make some provision for correcting them.

The best person to correct transactions in error is the person who made the error, and most often this is the person who coded the source document. This person is most familiar with the transaction, and the feedback of correcting errors makes for fewer of them. To correct the error, this person will need an error listing with which to work.

There are two ways to correct errors, by changing the bad transaction or by submitting a new one. Changing the original transaction is the most direct. Transactions on cards can be rekeypunched, transactions entered on a key to tape or disk device can be changed by data entry, and transactions submitted from an on-line terminal can be changed from the terminal.

The other method of correcting transactions in error is to discard the incorrect transaction and prepare a new one. In its simplest form, you ignore the rejected transactions and submit new ones. In a more sophisticated form, you place the rejected transactions into a separate file, an error suspense file. You then submit transactions against this file to cancel out the incorrect transaction and replace it with a correct one. This is similar to the way in which accountants make corrections by entering offsetting debits and credits. Accountants also like this method because it gives a complete audit trail. However, it requires what amounts to a separate update program.

Another variation in correcting errors is to combine the two previous methods. That is, you write the rejected transactions into an error suspense file, but then you change them directly in the file. The corrected transactions are resubmitted, and any resulting errors are again corrected. Errors are thus recycled until they are all corrected.

The availability and power of computer text editing systems provide a convenient tool for correcting errors and recycling them. If a text editing system, such as WYLBUR, is available which can operate on standard records, it can operate directly on the rejected transactions. When the corrections have been noted on the error listing, the text editor changes the trans-

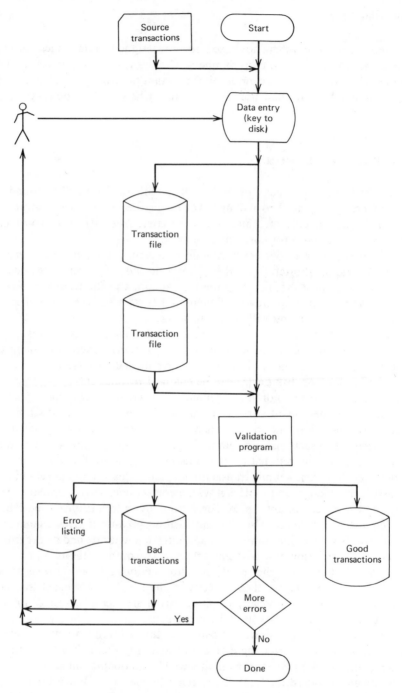

Figure 3 System flow for recycling errors.

actions in the error file. The terminal can be made available to the people who prepared the source document so that they can make the correction themselves.

After the transactions are corrected, they are run through the validation program and merged with the good transactions. This process is continued until no transactions are found in error. Not only does this simplify error corrections, but it also minimizes the elapsed time, which is important in a tight closing schedule. Corrections do not have to be resubmitted through data entry, and only the transactions in error are reprocessed.

When the transactions are changed from a terminal, there is no audit trail of the change as there would be if a transaction were prepared to correct the error. However, the transactions can be listed before and after they hve been corrected to establish the audit trail. The corrections penciled in on the error listing also form part of the audit trail. The system flow in Figure 3 illustrates the recycling of errors.

When a batch error occurs, the entire batch must be rejected. The simplest way to do this when errors are recycled is to read all the transactions belonging to a batch into a table, validating each transaction individually as it is read in. When the batch total is read, all the transactions can be written out as valid records if the batch total checks and if no errors were found on individual transactions. Otherwise the entire batch is written into the reject file.

REFORMATTING DATA

Date is often reformatted during validation. Transactions consisting of multiple physical records are combined into one record, and values obtained from tables or files may be picked up and added to the transaction to form the record. Numeric-character data is often converted into COMP-3 form.

Numeric data must often be transformed into COBOL format by replacing leading blanks with zeros. When data is entered by a data entry operator, such mundane matters as leading zeros and overpunching the sign can be done at input, but it is a different matter when data is entered from an on-line terminal by people who have not dedicated their life to serving the computer.

Imagine yourself trying to explain to a manager how to enter COBOL numbers from a terminal.

"It's easy," you say. "You just type the number."

The manager types 16.22 on the terminal.

"Oh yes," you say, "you can't type a decimal point. Just type the digits because the program has an assumed number of decimal points. Be sure to type the leading zeros, too."

"But how do I know how many decimal points each number has and how many leading zeros there are?" the manager asks.

"Well, you just have to know that," you say.

The manager types in −1622 on the terminal.

"Oh yes," you say, "you can't enter a minus sign. You have to overpunch over the rightmost digit."

"How do I overpunch on a terminal?" the manager asks, giving you a look best described as unkindly.

"Oh, that's right. You can't. Well it's not hard." You type in 162B on the terminal. "See, it's easy. You enter an alphabetic character: A is minus 1, B is minus 2, and so on. If you stick with it, you'll get it."

"I'd like to stick you with something," the manager says as he stalks away. "A million dollar computer and it can't handle the numbers I learned to write in grade school."

Sometimes for job security you must deal in COBOL with numbers such as −22 rather than 0002B.

The COBOL SIGN clause does permit a sign to be coded, but it must be in a fixed position in the field. The sign must also be present; COBOL does not assume an unsigned number to be plus when the SIGN clause is coded. The sign (+ or −) is carried as a separate leading or trailing character in numeric character data.

```
77  X    PIC S999 SIGN IS LEADING SEPARATE.
                         [X occupies four character positions]
        MOVE −14 TO X.   [X contains "−014"]
        MOVE 14 TO X.    [X contains "+014"]
```

But suppose that you want to read in signed or unsigned numbers with a floating left sign, and with a decimal point in a fixed position in the field. Assume that a card file contains numbers in columns 1 to 7 as:

bbb2.53
b−13.56
bb+7.24
bbb0.17

To read such numbers, first define an area into which the cards are to be read:

```
01  CARD-IN.
    05  CARD-NUM-PART    PIC 9(4).    [Leading digits]
    05  FILLER           PIC X.       [Decimal point]
    05  CARD-DEC-PART    PIC XX.      [Decimal digits]
    05  FILLER           PIC X(73).   [Pad out to 80 characters]
```

Then define an area to contain the number in character form:

```
01  EDIT-CHAR.
    05  EDIT-LEFT-HALF   PIC X(4).    [Leading digits]
    05  EDIT-RIGHT-HALF  PIC XX.      [Decimal digits]
01  EDIT-NUM REDEFINES EDIT-CHAR PIC S9(4)V99.
        □   □
    READ FILE-I INTO CARD-IN          [Read in a card]
        AT END done.
    MOVE CARD-NUM-PART TO EDIT-LEFT-HALF.
                            [Move numeric digits to get rid of decimal point]
    MOVE CARD-DEC-PART TO EDIT-RIGHT-HALF.
    EXAMINE EDIT-CHAR                  [Replace all blanks with
                                       zeros]
        REPLACING ALL SPACES BY ZEROS.
    EXAMINE EDIT-CHAR                  [Replace any plus sign
        REPLACING ALL "+" BY ZEROS.   with zeros and ignore
                                       it]
    EXAMINE EDIT-CHAR                  [Replace any minus sign
        TALLYING ALL "−"              with zero and count its
        REPLACING BY ZERO.            presence in TALLY]
    IF TALLY > ZERO                    [If number had a minus
        THEN COMPUTE EDIT-NUM =        sign, make it negative]
            − EDIT-NUM.
```

EDIT-NUM now contains the number, and arithmetic operations can be performed on it:

```
COMPUTE X = EDIT-NUM * 2.
```

It is more complex when the decimal point is not in a fixed position or if it might not appear, as in the numbers 0.0002, 25, −3.1, and 22.6645. The STRING statement must then be used to dissect the characters to construct the number. Such numbers may be uncommon in a computer production environment, but they are common when noncomputing people enter the numbers, such as for an on-line system.

GUIDELINES FOR VALIDATING

In designing the validation for a system, give consideration to the following points.

1 **Validate first, all in one place** All the validation for transactions should be done in a single program, as close to the point of origin as possible. There are systems in which transactions are passed on to several subsystems, with each subsystem validating the transactions according to its needs. The results are disastrous. A transaction is accepted in one place and rejected in another, and then the subsystems do not balance. If a change is made to a transaction, or a validation criterion is changed, finding all the places where validation is done becomes a major task.

   When you validate first, bad data is stopped before it gets into the system. When you validate in one place, it is easier to see what validation is done, it is easier to change the validation, and it ensures that transactions are acceptable to all subsystems before being accepted by any.

2 **Parameterize** The validation criterion is the most dynamic part of a system, and it will change more than California life styles. Use every tool at your disposal to minimize the impact of the change, including the use of tables read in from cards or files, using data items assigned initial values for validation limits and error messages, and whatever else can be conceived.

3 **Comment** The reasons for validating an item are not always apparent. Use comment statements to spell out the reasons. For example, if program statements verify that only certain employees charge to the undocumented entertainment expense account, use comments to explain the reason.

4 **Plan** Give as much thought to the validation as to the design of any other part of the system. You can often develop simple tools to aid in this, such as a decision table for validation. Using a form such as that shown in Figure 4 lets you analyze and specify the validation for each field.

5 **Catch all errors** Do not stop with the first error discovered in a transaction. Check for all possible errors before rejecting the transaction. This may result in some redundant error messages, but each pass through validation should catch all possible errors.

6 **Validate corrected transactions** The error rate will be higher for corrected transactions than for unedited transactions because the rejected

FIELD

NAME: _____

LENGTH: _____

DATA TYPE: _____

VALIDATION

SEQUENCE CHECK? _____

CLASS TEST? _____

PRESENCE REQUIRED? _____

FIELD DEPENDS ON FIELD: _____

SPECIFIC VALUES FIELD CAN CONTAIN: _____

RANGE CHECK.   MIN: _____   MAX: _____

TABLE LOOKUP IN FILE: _____

ACTION IF ERROR: _____

Figure 4 Typical validation form.

transactions are often problem transactions, and it may take two or three passes to get them right. Also there is usually a rush to get in the corrections, and this leads inevitably to errors. Validate all transactions after they are corrected as if they had never been entered.

Updating Direct-Access Files

Validation is usually separate from updating. The transactions are read and validated. Only when all the errors are corrected should the appropriate files be updated. Direct-access files are the exception. The transactions for them may be applied by the validation program. There are two reasons for this. First, a direct-access file allows individual records to be updated, and there is no need for a separate program to do the updating. You must access the file to validate, and having retrieved a record, you might as well make the change and write it back out. Second, the file may need to be updated immediately so that the transactions that follow can be validated. If an update contains a transaction to add a record and also a transaction to update the record, the second transaction will be rejected as being applied to a nonexistent record unless the first transaction creates a record in the file.

One word of warning. Whenever you update a direct-access file, you must have a means of restoring the file in the event that it is destroyed. This is discussed in the next chapter.

FIVE

Files

The transmission of data between memory and a file contained on an I/O device is often the most complex part of programming. It requires a knowledge of the data to be transmitted, the hardware devices, their physical capacity, and the language features. But the real difficulty is the subtle logic required to process and update files.

FILE STORAGE

Most files are contained on either cards, tape, or disk, each with its own unique features.

Cards

Punched cards are the universal I/O medium, and most programs and much of their data originate on cards, or more properly, on card images. Cards are becoming more of a concept than a physical entity. Card input is often keyed directly onto tape or disk, and so when we speak of card input, we are actually referring to card images. A punched card contains 80 characters, whereas card images produced on key to tape or disk devices usually allow more.

The drawbacks of punched cards are that they are relatively slow to read and punch, are awkward and bulky to handle, cannot be rewritten, and can contain only 80 characters.

Although the punched card is rapidly going the way of large cars and affordable gasoline, it still has its moments. Punched cards can be interpreted, so that a person can read the data punched on the card, something not possible with tape or disk. Card decks are portable, and they are the only type of file that you can toss in your desk and forget about. They are relatively indestructible, and no one will hound you to release your storage as they will if you retain tape or disk files. Card I/O is sequential, but cards can be updated directly by hand, eliminating complex file update programs for simple applications.

Magnetic Tape

Tape is the high-volume storage medium. A full 2400 foot reel of magnetic tape is equivalent in storage to 672,897 cards when blocked at 800 bytes per block and 6250 bits per inch.

Tapes are not a shareable storage medium. If you request a tape, you get the entire 2400 feet, even if you plan to use only a few feet. (Tapes get shorter with age. The first few feet often become worn, and the operators may strip this part off when the tape is recycled.) Tapes are a reusable resource, and can be rewritten over and over again. Tapes, like cards, can contain only sequential files.

A single file can be stored across several tape reels, so that an unlimited amount of information can actually be contained. Alternatively, several files can be stored on a single tape reel by separating them with file marks. Tapes cannot be opened for input and output concurrently. This means that you cannot rewrite individual records within a tape file. You can, however, rewrite an entire file on tape. If a file is rewritten, any following file on that tape reel is destroyed. Thus if a tape contains three files and the second file is rewritten, the first file is unchanged, but the third file is destroyed. Tapes are updated by reading the old tape and applying any changes to produce a new tape. An automatic backup is obtained by keeping the old tape and the changes.

Blocks written on a tape are separated by an interblock gap, which is a length of blank tape about $\frac{1}{4}$ inch long. The end of file is marked by a 3.6 inch gap, followed by a file or tape mark. The following formula shows how to compute the length of tape required to store a given number of records:

$$\text{length} = (\text{number of records}) \times \frac{\text{blocksize}/\text{density} + k}{12 \times (\text{records per block})}$$

where

$\qquad$ length $=$ Length of tape in feet required to store the records.

$\quad$ blocksize $=$ Length of block in bytes.

$\qquad$ density $=$ Bits per inch: 200, 556, 800, 1600, or 6250. (If there is a choice, use the highest because it is faster, allows more storage, and is more reliable due to the more advanced hardware features.)

$\qquad\qquad k =$ Interblock gap in inches: 0.75 for 7-track, 0.6 for 9-track, except for 6250 bits per inch, when it is 0.3.

For example, if 400 byte records with 10 records per block are stored on a 9-track, 1600 bit per inch tape, the length required to store 100,000 records is computed as follows:

$$\text{length} = 100 \times \frac{4000/1600 + 0.6}{12 \times 10} = 2583.3 \text{ feet}$$

Since a single tape reel contains 2400 feet, two reels would be required to contain this file.

Tape makes excellent long-term storage because a reel of tape is relatively inexpensive and can contain a great deal of information in a small storage space. Tapes are considerably faster to process than cards and may be faster or slower than direct-access storage, depending upon the particular device.

Tapes must be mounted by an operator, which increases the job's turnaround time. The number of tape reels that can be simultaneously processed depends upon the number of tape units on the computer. Tape mounting can often be minimized by placing multiple files on the same tape reel. However, rewinding tapes and spacing back and forth between files is time consuming, so careful thought should be given to the order of the files on tape.

Direct-Access Storage Devices

Direct access, the most versatile storage device, can contain sequential, direct, relative, and indexed files. Direct-access storage derives its name from the way data is accessed. Unlike tape or cards, we need not read the preceding records to get to a specific record. Direct-access storage generally consists of disks and drums, with disk devices being the most prevalent.

A disk device consists of a stack of rotating recording surfaces similar to a stack of phonograph records. Each disk surface has many concentric tracks radiating inward toward the center, each containing the same amount of data. A set of electronic read/write heads is positioned between each disk surface and connected to an access arm. When a specific track is read or written, the access arm moves to position the read/write head over the track. The read/write head looks for a special marker on the rotating track to tell it where the track begins. Thus there are two physical delays in accessing a specific track: a seek delay which depends on how far the access arm must be moved, and a rotational delay which averages out to be half a revolution.

Since there is a read/write head for each disk surface, several tracks can be read without arm movement. The tracks that lie one on top of the other form an imaginary cylinder in which all the tracks are accessible without arm movement. Some disk drives have a read/write head for each track, which eliminates the seek.

Disks are the most versatile storage device because of their large storage capacity and speed. Many disk devices have removable packs, allowing a disk unit to contain an infinite amount of data, but an installation generally controls the use of private or mountable packs. It requires a few minutes for the operator to change disk packs, and not only are the disk packs relatively heavy, but also if dropped they can be destroyed. Tape reels are more convenient to mount than disk packs.

A drum is similar to a disk, except that it contains a single cylinder of tracks, each with its own read/write head. The seek delay is thus eliminated, and the rotational delay is minimal because of the drum's high rotational speed. Drums generally contain less data than disks, but they are considerably faster. They are used for small, frequently used files, usually portions of the operating system.

Direct-access storage devices are reusable resources and may be rewritten many times. It is possible to delete a disk or drum file, allowing the space to be reallocated and reused. Alternatively, you can overwrite the data in an existing file. Both disks and drums are relatively expensive storage. They can give immediate access if the pack is already mounted, which is important in on-line applications. They are generally used for temporary files, frequently used files, and must be used for direct, relative, and indexed files. Disks and drums are sharable. Several people may store files on the same volume.

Many systems require you to specify the amount of disk space to allocate to each file, and the program will be terminated if the requested space is unavailable or if the program exceeds the space allocated. Estimating the disk space is difficult, particularly when a file grows over time. In multiprogramming systems where many users share the same disk packs, there is no easy way to tell when a job is submitted whether enough space will be available. In a production job you can make the first job step allocate all the direct-access storage space to ensure that enough is available for all job steps.

DESIGNING THE FILES

Minimizing the Impact of Change

Business applications are heavily I/O oriented, and you should carefully select the proper I/O device for each file. Specify as little about the I/O device as possible within the program, leaving such details to the JCL. By doing this, a different I/O device can be used or a blocking factor changed without modifying the program. Then if a disk file grows in size, requiring it to be moved to tape, or if a tape unit is changed to one of higher density, or if a program is tested with card data and then used to process card images on tape during production, the program does not need to be recompiled.

Allow ample extra space for growth in files since files tend to grow. Exceeding the file space is expensive, because a program can run for hours before its file space is exceeded and the program terminated. Production jobs are often run on off shifts and there are more pleasant things to do at night than to try to repair a run lost through insufficient file space.

In addition to allowing extra space in a file for more records, allow extra space within a record to add new fields. Over time, new data items will need to be added to records. By leaving extra space within a record to contain these new data items, the data can be added without affecting the programs that access the file.

For some reason we programmers are loath to allow extra space in either files or records. In engineering a safety factor of 2 or 3 is expected in design, but programmers will often begrudge a few extra bytes in a record or a few extra tracks in a disk file. This is specious economy. If an application cannot afford a safety factor, then the application should be scrapped. This may sound harsh, but a quick termination of an application that cannot be successful is merciful.

All programs referencing a file should use the same file and record descriptions. In COBOL, place the file and record descriptions in a library and use the COPY statement to copy them into any program referencing the file. Then when a file is changed, the change can be made for all programs that reference the file by recompiling them.

Efficiency

Data can be transmitted very quickly between memory and direct-access devices or magnetic tapes once the transmission of data begins. However, it takes quite long, relative to the computer's speed, to start the transmission because of mechanical inertia and, for direct-access devices, the time to position the access arm over the proper track and the time to rotate the track around to the start of the block. Blocking allows large, efficient groups of data to be transmitted at one time. Many installations charge the job on the basis of blocks transmitted, and large blocks can significantly reduce the run costs. Blocking also conserves storage space on the I/O device by limiting the number of interblock gaps.

For a reasonably well written program, the blocking for sequential files will have more impact on the efficiency than any other factor. Block as high as possible within the constraints of the memory size and the I/O devices. If a record containing 100 characters is blocked at 50 records per block, each block will contain 5000 characters, and for two buffers it will require a total of 10,000 bytes for the I/O buffers. For disks select a block size close to the track size or some even fraction of the track size so that the blocks are stored on a track without wasting space.

Backup

In designing the backup of files, make the assumption that any file can be destroyed at any time. If a system runs for any length of time, this assumption will prove justified. If there is no means of restoring the file, you may contribute to the unemployment problem. As mentioned, backup is more critical for random-access files than for sequential files because updating a random-access file changes the contents of the original file.

Three levels of backup are customarily retained: the current file, the previous file, and the next previous file—but the level of backup depends upon the criticality of the application. Do not forget that whatever destroys the original file might also destroy the backup. As an extreme example, if a fire destroys an old master, it will likely destroy the backup copies if they are kept at the same physical location. Critical applications should have off-site storage of the backup copies.

Files are backed up either by copying them or by retaining the files that went into their creation. If you are updating an old sequential file with transactions to create a new file, you can back up either by copying the new file or by retaining the old file and the transactions file. For systems that run frequently, such as on-line systems, the backup is generally done at fixed time intervals, also saving all the transactions applied during the interval. Backup files are usually placed on tape because of its low cost and high capacity.

Many installations back up their on-line direct-access storage devices on a daily or weekly basis, and this provides a degree of protection. However, it may be difficult to restore a single file. You should assume the responsibilty of backup for your systems.

One of the weaknesses in many backup systems is that they either do not work or they are difficult to make work. A system can be dutifully backing up a file for a year before something goes wrong and the file needs to be restored. Then it is discovered that no program is available to restore the file, or that the backup file has been written incorrectly and cannot be used. Do not back up files without providing a means of restoring them and making sure that it works.

One way to back up a system which uses random-access files is to copy the files to direct-access storage as the first step in the job, and then to copy each random-access file to tape after it has been updated. Several files can be stacked on a tape reel. This technique works well for systems that are run periodically with fairly long periods between runs.

There are several advantages to backing up random-access files on tape as sequential files and restoring them to direct-access storage before a run. It ensures that the backup system is working, it automatically reorganizes indexed files, it releases direct-access storage space when it is not needed, and it makes backing up and restoring the files routine.

Checkpoint/Restart

Many operating systems provide a checkpoint/restart facility. Checkpoints consist of a snapshot of a program's status at selected points during execution so that if the program terminates for some reason, the run can be restarted from the last checkpoint rather than from the beginning of the run. The COBOL checkpoint occurs after a specified number of records have been read or written for a file or when the end of a tape or disk volume is reached.

Checkpoints are done because of the potential cost or time limitations of restarting a large program. The checkpoints themselves are expensive, complex, and you may not always be able to successfully restart the run anyway. Restarting does no good if the problem is caused by bad data or a program error. Checkpoints are more a protection against hardware and operating system errors than protection against application program or data errors.

The main problem with the checkpoint/restart facility in computer operating systems is that it is too complicated. It is difficult to understand and use, and it is difficult to verify that it will work properly when needed. If you can get by without it, do so.

Unless you have an extremely long-running job step, you probably will not need to use the checkpoint/restart facility. You can design the job to be able to restart from a particular job step. The design of any production system should allow restarting from selected job steps, even if it is only the first step.

Files on direct-access storage devices cause the most difficulty in restarting from a job step, especially temporary files that are deleted after the job step is run. By knowing beforehand the requirement to restart from selected job steps, temporary files can be retained until the run is verified. The steps in a production system might be the following:

JOB 1.

STEP 1   Allocate space on the direct-access storage devices for the files.

STEP 2   Restore any direct-access storage device files from tape.

STEP 3 Run the job steps, retaining all files on direct-access storage devices that may be necessary for restart.

STEP 4 Back up the direct-access files onto tape.

Manually verify that the run is correct.

JOB 2.

STEP 1 Scratch the files on direct-access storage devices.

On the subject of setting up production runs, you often need to enter control information for an individual program and for a system. For a program you might want to enter a request for debugging information or trigger a particular option in a report. For a system you might want to enter the period end date and various control parameters, such as a year-end flag to request year-end reports, or a quarter start flag to reset quarterly files to zero.

Control information can be given to a program through the JCL in some systems, or it can be read in from control cards. For a system where several programs may need the date and control information, it is better to place the information in a direct-access file so that all programs can have easy access to it. The first job step in a system might write this information into a direct-access file for subsequent use by all the other programs in the system.

SIX

Sequential Files

Sequential files are used more than any other file organization, and cards, tapes, and disk can contain them. The sequential file organization is also the simplest.

SEQUENTIAL ACCESS

The records in a sequential file must be read in the order they are physically stored, and physically stored in the order they are written. Sequential access is best when all the records in a file must be processed, and for this it is the fastest access method. For example, sequential access is efficient for processing all the records in a payroll file. But locating a single employee in a personnel file is relatively inefficient because all records up to the desired employee must be read first.

Although the records must be processed in the order they are stored, they can be placed into a desired order by sorting. For example, a social security file could be sorted on age in descending order if there were a need to make social security payments to the oldest people first, in the event that social security goes bankrupt.

With sequential access, the same file cannot be used for concurrent input and output. (The rewrite feature is an exception and is discussed later.) If you want to change a single record in an existing file, you must read all the records in the file up to the record to be changed, writing them into a new file. Then read the record to be changed, change it; write it into the new file, and read the remaining records in the old file, writing them into the new file. Essentially the same process is necessary to add or delete records.

This may seem like a lot of effort to change one lone record, but the fact that you cannot change the file you are reading does have one important benefit. You are automatically left with a backup—the old input file. If you need to rerun the job for some reason, and you surely will, you simply resubmit it with the old input file. As we shall see later with the direct-access method, it is not this simple when you change records in the input file.

With sequential access a few other hardware features are sometimes provided. Some computers allow tape files to be read backwards. At open, the system positions the tape file to the end-of-file position, and then retrieves each record by backing up the tape. The effect of this is to reverse the sort order. In our social security file, if we wanted to process the file based on age in ascending order, we could use the file already sorted on age in descending order and read it backwards. In practice, however, you will probably never read a tape backwards.

Some systems also provide the rewrite feature for sequential files stored on direct-access devices. This feature allows you to read a record and then rewrite it to update it in place with sequential access. But again, if you update in place, you need to give careful consideration to your file recovery.

SEQUENTIAL LOGIC

The three operations performed on sequential files are to write them, a record at a time, to read them, a record at a time, and to sort them. A separate chapter is devoted to sorting. Here we concentrate on reading and writing sequential files.

Copy

The main problem in a copy is how to handle the end-of-file. Although a copy is perhaps the simplest file operation, there are hundreds of ways to code one. A decade ago the copy might have been coded like this:

```
START-COPY.
        READ INPUT-FILE INTO INPUT-RECORD
            AT END GO TO COPY-DONE.
        WRITE OUTPUT-RECORD FROM INPUT-RECORD.
        GO TO START-COPY.
COPY-DONE.
```

Today such a program is considered the epitome of bad coding because the GO TOs make the coding difficult to follow and difficult to modify. A simple example such as this does not do justice to the problems caused by GO TOs, but when you modify a program containing many of them, you will be convinced.

Today the copy would be done using structured programming constructs, either the DO WHILE or the DO UNTIL. The pseudocode is as follows:

1 Using the DO WHILE

Set end-of-file flag.
Do while not end-of-file.
    Read input-file into input-record.
    If not end-of-file
        then write output-record from input-record.
End.

2 Using the DO UNTIL

Do until end-of-file.
    Read input-file into input-record.
    If not end-of-file
        then write output-record from input-record.
End.

The DO WHILE and DO UNTIL differ only in that the DO WHILE conditional test is performed before the loop is executed so that the statements within the loop may not be executed even once. The conditional test is performed at the end of the DO UNTIL loop so that the statements within the loop are always executed at least once. In COBOL, the PERFORM UNTIL acts as a DO WHILE, whereas there is no direct form of the DO UNTIL. For this reason, and because the DO WHILE works better than the DO UNTIL for I/O loops anyway, the DO WHILE is used here.

The previous examples also illustrate the technique of writing pseudocode. Pseudocode is a language that you make up, preferably using the structured programming constructs, which approximates the programming language you will use, but which is free of any arbitrary constraints. It is a tool used as an intermediate step between your thinking and the actual coding. It often replaces the need for flow charts and structured diagrams for program design. Since the pseudocode is read only by you, you are free to make it do what you wish, to design it for your own needs, and to put it into the form that helps you most. It remains to translate the pseudocode into COBOL. The DO WHILE can be coded as follows. (For simplicity, the opens and closes are omitted.)

```
        MOVE "NO" TO EOF-INPUT-FILE.
        PERFORM COPY-FILE UNTIL EOF-INPUT-FILE = "YES".
            □   □
COPY-FILE.
```

```
      READ INPUT-FILE INTO INPUT-RECORD
          AT END MOVE "YES" TO EOF-INPUT-FILE.
      IF EOF-INPUT-FILE = "NO"
          THEN WRITE OUTPUT-RECORD FROM INPUT-RECORD.
**** EXIT
```

Another way of coding the loop is to use a "prime" read. That is, read the first record outside the loop to "prime" it so that the loop is entered with the first record already read. Since the loop is entered with the first record read, no test for end-of-file is needed before writing out the record. The prime read simplifies the programming by eliminating the logic necessary to account for the fact that there is no record the first time through the loop.

```
      MOVE "NO" TO EOF-INPUT-FILE.
      READ INPUT-FILE INTO INPUT-RECORD
          AT END MOVE "YES" TO EOF-INPUT-FILE.
      PERFORM COPY-FILE UNTIL EOF-INPUT-FILE = "YES".
          □  □
  COPY-FILE.
      WRITE OUTPUT-RECORD FROM INPUT-RECORD.
      READ INPUT-FILE INTO INPUT-RECORD
          AT END MOVE "YES" TO EOF-INPUT-FILE.
**** EXIT
```

Note that the loop is not executed at all if there is an immediate end-of-file, and that placing the READ at the end of the loop causes the loop to terminate when an end-of-file is encountered.

Some people react almost violently to there being more than one READ statement per file in a program. While it is true that READ statements should not be scattered all over a program, there is nothing wrong about placing a READ statement, or any statement for that matter including a GO TO, where it is functionally needed. One way to have a single READ statement per file is to PERFORM the READ. While there may be virtue to replacing two READ statements with two PERFORM statements and adding a paragraph containing the READ, the benefits are less apparent. However, there are often several statements associated with the READ statements for a file to perform sequence checking and count records. For this it is best to place the READ and its associated statements in a paragraph and PERFORM them.

Sequence Checking

With sequence checking we encounter the look ahead and look back problem. Many times in processing a file, you need to look ahead at the next record or look back at the previous record to determine what must be done with the current record. To check the sequence of an input file, we must look back at each previous record to see if the current record is in the proper sequence.

For illustration we will sequence check the copy program already illustrated. Assume that the file records are to be in ascending order on a field named INPUT-RECORD-KEY. The pseudocode is as follows:

```
Set first-time flag.
Set end-of-file flag.
Do while not end-of-file.
    If first-time
        then reset first-time flag
        else if (input-record-key not > old-input-record-key)
            then error—out of sequence.
    Read input-file into input-record.
    If not end-of-file
        then write output-record from input-record
            move input-record to old-input-record.
    End.
```

The coding is simplified by using a "prime" read. This eliminates both the end-of-file and the first-time condition tests.

```
Set end-of-file flag.
Read input-file into input-record.
Do while not end-of-file.
    Write output-record from input-record.
    Move input-record to old-input-record.
    Read input-file into input-record.
    If not end-of-file
        then if (input-record-key not > old-input-record-key)
            then error—out of sequence.
    End.
```

This pseudocode translates into COBOL as follows:

```
        MOVE "NO" TO   EOF-INPUT-FILE.
        READ INPUT-FILE INTO INPUT-RECORD
            AT END MOVE "YES" TO EOF-INPUT-FILE.
        PERFORM COPY-FILE UNTIL EOF-INPUT-FILE = "YES".
            □   □
COPY-FILE.
        WRITE OUTPUT-RECORD FROM INPUT-RECORD.
        MOVE INPUT-RECORD TO OLD-INPUT-RECORD.
        READ INPUT-FILE INTO INPUT-RECORD
            AT END MOVE "YES" TO EOF-INPUT-FILE.
        IF EOF-INPUT-FILE = "NO"
            THEN IF (INPUT-RECORD-KEY NOT > OLD-INPUT-
                                            RECORD-KEY)
                    THEN error—out of sequence.
**** EXIT
```

Summarizing

Summarizing also has the look ahead and look back problem. In summarizing, all records having identical record keys (or any field upon which the records are sorted) are summed or combined into a single record. The pseudocode for this is as follows:

Set end-of-file flag.
Read input-file into input-record.
Initialize summarized-record.
Do while not end-of-file.
    Sum input-record-fields into summarized-record-fields.
    Save input-record as old-input-record.
    Read input-file into input-record.
    If (input-record-key not = old-input-record-key) or (end-of-file)
        then write output-record from summarized-record
                initialize summarized-record.
    If not end-of-file
        then if (input-record-key not > old-input-record-key)
                then error—out of sequence.
End.

This translates into COBOL as:

```
        MOVE "NO" TO EOF-INPUT-FILE.
        READ INPUT-FILE INTO CURRENT-RECORD
            AT END MOVE "YES" TO EOF-INPUT-FILE.
        MOVE ZEROS TO SUMMARIZED-RECORD-FIELDS.
        MOVE INPUT-RECORD-KEY TO SUMMARIZED-
                                    RECORD-KEY.
        PERFORM SUMMARIZE-INPUT-FILE
            UNTIL (EOF-INPUT-FILE = "YES").
            □   □
SUMMARIZE-INPUT-FILE.
        ADD INPUT-RECORD-FIELDS TO SUMMARIZED-
                                    RECORD-FIELDS.
        MOVE INPUT-RECORD TO OLD-INPUT-RECORD.
        READ INPUT-FILE INTO INPUT-RECORD
            AT END MOVE "YES" TO EOF-INPUT-FILE.
        IF (INPUT-RECORD-KEY NOT = OLD-INPUT-RECORD-
                                    KEY) OR
            (EOF-INPUT-FILE = "YES")
            THEN WRITE OUTPUT-FILE FROM SUMMARIZED-
                                    RECORD
                MOVE ZEROS TO SUMMARIZED-RECORD-
                                    FIELDS
                MOVE INPUT-RECORD-KEY TO
                                    SUMMARIZED-RECORD-KEY.
        IF EOF-INPUT-FILE = "NO"
            THEN IF (INPUT-RECORD-KEY NOT > OLD-INPUT-
                                    RECORD-KEY)
                THEN error—out of sequence.
****  EXIT
```

Another technique that simplifies the logic is to eliminate the end-of-file flag and instead set the record key to HIGH-VALUES to indicate an end-of-file and to LOW-VALUES for the first-time flag. Besides eliminating separate flags, this simplifies the logic of sequence checking. The pseudocode for summarizing with this technique would look as follows:

```
Move low-values to old-input-record-key.
Read input-file into input-record
        at end move high-values to input-record-key.
Initialize summarized-record.
Do while input-record-key not = high-values.
        Sum input-record-fields into output-record-fields.
```

Save input-record as old-input-record.
Read input-file into input-record
    at end move high-values to input-record-key.
If (input-record-key not = old-input-record-key)
  then write output-record from summarized-record
    zero summarized-record-fields.
If (input-record-key not > old-input-record-key)
  then error—out of sequence.
End.

The use of high and low values works only if the record key cannot contain either as a legitimate value. Since numeric fields might well contain either high or low values, it should not be used in the rare event that the record key is numeric. But for alphanumeric fields high or low values are unlikely because they are not valid characters and cannot be keyed from input. One can argue that there is a possibility of any field containing any value for source input, and this is true. However, the probability is low. There is a finite probability that you will be trampled to death by a lovesick elephant on the way to work, but the probability is so small that you can safely ignore it. So if you survived the risk of being flattened by a flirtatious elephant, you can probably face the risk with its even lower probability that an alphanumeric field will contain high or low values.

Updating

With sequential updating, an old master file is updated by reading it sequentially and applying transactions to it from another sequential file (a transactions file). The result is an updated or new master file. The records in the old master file and transactions file are matched on their record keys, and both files must be in sort order on the key.

The updating consists of adding, deleting, replacing, or changing records. The following logic errors can occur:

- **Add**   Error if the record already exists in the old master file or if there are duplicate transactions.
- **Delete**   Error if the record does not exist in the old master file or if there are duplicate transactions.
- **Replace**   Error if the record does not exist in the old master file. Duplicate transactions may or may not be allowed.
- **Change**   Error if the record does not exist in the old master file. Duplicate transactions are usually allowed.

There are two ways to do a sequential update: to read the master file and apply the transactions to it, or to read the transactions file and apply the master file to it. The difference between the two methods is shown as follows.

Applying transactions to master:

1   Get next master.
2   Process all transactions less than master, writing out adds.
3   Process all transactions equal to master, changing, replacing, or deleting master.
4   Write master unless deleted.
5   Continue with step 1.

Applying master to transactions:

1   Get next transaction.
2   Process all master less than transaction, writing out master.
3   Process all transactions less than master, writing out adds.
4   Process all transactions equal to master, changing, replacing, or deleting master.
5   Write master unless deleted.
6   Continue with step 1.

Since the update is simpler if the transactions are applied to the master file, we shall use this method. For our update procedure, the replace is omitted because it is done in the same manner as a change, and we can also accomplish the replace by a delete followed by an add. The update is to handle the following situations:

•   The add, change, and delete can be in any order and will be handled properly. That is, if we change and then delete, we delete the changed record. If we delete and then change, the record to be changed will not be found, resulting in an error.
•   Multiple transactions can be applied to the master. Several change transactions can be applied to the same master record, or the master record can be changed and deleted.
•   We can change or delete an added transaction.

The last requirement that we allow an added transaction to be changed or deleted makes the update a little more difficult, but it can be done by treating an add transaction as if it were a master file record just read in. For this, we need to modify our basic update procedure.

1 Get first master.
2 Process all transactions less than the master. If add, save master, and make transaction the current master.
3 Process all transactions equal to the current master, changing, replacing, or deleting.
4 Write the current master unless deleted.
5 If a master record was saved, restore it as the current master; otherwise get next master.
6 Continue with step 2.

So far we have made the assumption that there is one master file, one transactions file, and that a transaction is to apply to a single master record. This is almost always the case. If there are several transactions files, it is best to merge the transactions (this may have to be done inside the program if the files have different formats) and treat them as a single transactions file. If there are several master files, it is best to use the second method of updating—to read the transactions file and apply the master records to it; again merging the master file records so that the program is written as if there were a single file. If there are multiple transactions and multiple master files, it becomes too complicated to think about.

If a single transactions record is to be applied to several master file records, it is best to store any such transactions in a table until all appropriate master file records have been updated.

Ignoring these complications, we now examine how to program a single transactions file applied to a single master file. To illustrate the update, we contrast four tools that are often used to design programs: the structured diagram, the flow chart, the decision table, and the pseudocode.

With the first tool, the structured diagram, the update would appear as in Figure 5. The structured diagram excels at laying out the overall structure of a program, ignoring detail where you want. While it is good at showing structure, it is poor at showing sequence and detail. Thus with a structured diagram you can easily tell how the program is organized, but often it is a little difficult to tell exactly what it does. It makes good documentation because it is easy to change and reflects the program's structure, which may be poorly done in the source code. However, structured diagrams usually do not contain enough detail to answer questions, which is one of the main uses of documentation.

The second tool, a flowchart of the update, would appear as shown in Figure 6. It is good at showing sequence and detail, but poor at showing

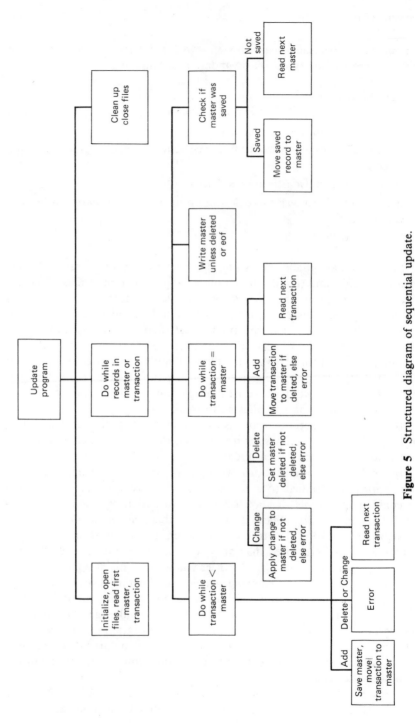

Figure 5 Structured diagram of sequential update.

84

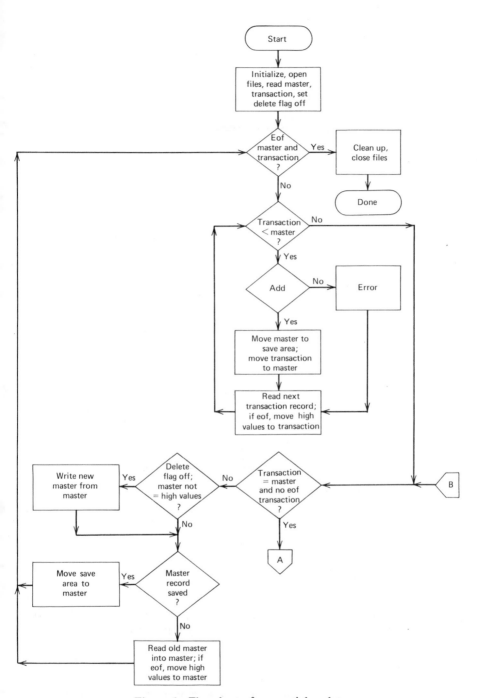

Figure 6 Flowchart of sequential update.

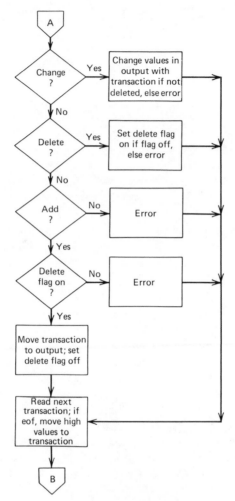

Figure 6 Continued.

structure. With the flowchart it is hard to ignore detail. Its strength is in complex, detailed logic. Its weakness is in laying out an overall design in broad strokes. It is poor for documentation because it is redundant to the source code and is difficult to change.

The third tool is a decision table. It is most useful when there is a binary choice, yes or no, for each combination of events. Its advantage is that it is concise, easy to draw, serves to remind you of the action required for each possible outcome, and is good for both design and documentation. Its disadvantage is that it shows neither structure nor sequence. It works best to supplement one of the other methods. Decision tables often seem mysterious, but in fact they are so commonplace that we scarcely recognize when we are using them. Only when they are given rigorous definition do they become forbidding. Figure 7 illustrates a decision table.

The fourth design tool is the pseudocode. Its advantage is that it resembles the final coding in the computer language, and that you are free to go to whatever level of detail you want. It shows detail, structure, and sequence. The disadvantage of the pseudocode is that if you do not discipline yourself, you can go into too much detail and end up essentially writing the program. The pseudocode is poor as documentation because no one but you may be able to understand it, and because it becomes redundant to the source coding.

There is no absolute rule as to which design tool to use. You might use all four for a complicated program, and use none for a simple one. You might use one of them for only a portion of a program. When it is you who is designing the program, you should be free to use whatever works best for you. Whatever you use should not be an exercise in rote effort, as often occurs with flowcharts.

The pseudocode for the update program that follows is but one of several ways of programming it. The goal here is to use as few flags as possible. The use of flags is minimized because they make it hard to follow the program; to understand the action taken in one place in the program requires you to know what happened somewhere else.

```
Read trans-file into trans-record
      at end move high-values to trans-record.
Read old-master into master-record
      at end move high-values to master-record.
Do while no eof both files.
    Set master-saved flag off.
    Do while trans-record < master-record.
        If (trans is add)
            then move master-record to save-area
                 move trans-record to master-record
                 set master-saved flag on
            else error—delete or change to record not there, transaction
                 ignored.
        Read trans-file into trans-record
            at end move high-values to trans-record.
    End.
    Set delete flag off.
    Do while (trans-record = master-record) and
              (no eof trans-file).
```

	Old Master					
	No end-of-file			End-of-file		
	Action to take	Transaction	Old master	Action to take	Transaction	Old master
Transactions End-of-file	Write current master unless deleted	No	Yes	Done	No	No
< Master Add	Save old master, make add current master	Yes	No	Make add current master	Yes	No
Change	Error	Yes	No	Error	Yes	No
Delete	Error	Yes	No	Error	Yes	No
= Master Add	Error	Yes	No	—	—	—
Change	Apply change unless delete flag on	Yes	No	—	—	—
Delete	Flag as deleted	Yes	No	—	—	—
> Master	Write current master unless deleted	No	Yes*	—	—	—

Figure 7   Decision table for sequential update.

*Unless old master saved—then restore.

```
        If (trans is change)
            then if delete flag off
                    then change master-record with trans-record
                    else error—changing deleted record
        Else if (trans is delete)
            then if delete flag off
                    then set delete flag on
                    else error—deleting deleted record
        Else if (trans is add)
            then if delete flag on
                    then move trans-record to master-record
                        set delete flag off
                    else error—adding record already there
        Else error—update action not add, change, delete.
        Read trans-file into trans-record
            at end move high-values to trans-record.
        End.
    If (delete flag off) and
    (master-record not = high-values)
    then write new-master from master-record.
    If master-saved flag on
        then move save-area to master-record
        else if no eof master-file
                then read master-file into master-record
                    at end move high-values to master-record.
End.
```

Now let us translate this code into COBOL. But before beginning, we should develop the full specifications for the program. For brevity, we will omit validation of the transaction data fields and printing the run statistics.

1 Old master file

- File name: OLD-MASTER.
- Record is: 01   MASTER-RECORD.
                    05   MASTER-KEY is record key.
                    05   MASTER-FIELDS are data fields.
- Should be in ascending sequence on MASTER-KEY.
- Should be no duplicate records

2 Transaction File

- File name: TRANS-FILE.
- Record: 01   TRANS-RECORD.

05 TRANS-KEY is record key.

05 TRANS-ACTION tells action. The actions are made parameters: ADD-ACTION for add, CHANGE-ACTION for change, and DELETE-ACTION for delete. This way the program can easily be modified to handle any mnemonic code for the actions.

05 TRANS-FIELDS are data fields.

- Should be in ascending order on TRANS-KEY and TRANS-AC-TION. The add, change, and delete actions can be in any predetermined order.
- Add transactions

  Should be no duplicate transactions.

  Must not already be in master file.

  Can add after deleting a record.

- Change transactions

  Can be duplicate changes to same record.

  Must match a record in master file or a previous add transaction.

  Can change an added record.

- Delete transactions

  Can be no duplicate transactions.

  Must match record in master file or a previous add transaction.

  Can delete an added record.

3 **New master file**

- File name: NEW-MASTER.
- Record: 01 NEW-MASTER-RECORD.

4 **Save-area record**

- Record: 01 SAVE-AREA.
  05 SAVE-KEY is record key.
  05 SAVE-FIELDS are data fields.

5 **Program statistics**

- MASTER-IN-COUNT contains count of master records read.
- TRANS-COUNT contains count of transactions read.
- TRANS-ERROR-COUNT contains count of transactions in error.
- MASTER-OUT-COUNT contains count of new master records written.

6   Flags

- MASTER-SAVE-FLAG contains "N" if master record not saved; contains "Y" if master record saved.

- MASTER-DELETED-FLAG contains "N" if master record not deleted; contains "Y" if master record deleted.

- GOOD-TRANSACTION-FLAG contains "N" if transaction not good; contains "Y" if transaction is good.

All the records are assumed to be described in the WORKING-STORAGE section. The COBOL coding is as follows:

```
MOVE LOW-VALUES TO PREVIOUS-TRANS-KEY,
                   PREVIOUS-TRANS-ACTION,
                   PREVIOUS-MASTER-KEY.
    [We initialize some fields used for sequence checking]
PERFORM B00-GET-NEXT-MASTER-RECORD.
PERFORM C00-GET-NEXT-TRANSACTION.
    [A 'prime' READ is used for both files; the READs are placed in paragraphs be-
    cause the paragraphs also check the sequence, and are invoked from a couple of
    places]
PERFORM A00-UPDATE-MASTER
        UNTIL (TRANS-KEY = HIGH-VALUES) AND
              (MASTER-KEY = HIGH-VALUES).
    [This is the Do while no-eof-both-files]
    □   □
A00-UPDATE-MASTER.
    [Here to process all transactions while we have a master record]
MOVE "N" TO MASTER-SAVED-FLAG.
    [This flag tells us whether we saved a master record]
PERFORM A-10-TRANS-KEY-LOW
        UNTIL (TRANS-KEY NOT < MASTER-KEY).
MOVE "N" TO MASTER-DELETED-FLAG.
    [This flag tells us if we have deleted a master file record]
PERFORM A20-TRANS-EQUAL-MASTER
        UNTIL (TRANS-KEY NOT = MASTER-KEY) OR
              (TRANS-KEY = HIGH-VALUES).
IF (MASTER-DELETED-FLAG = "NO") AND
   (MASTER-KEY NOT = HIGH-VALUES)
   THEN WRITE NEW-MASTER FROM MASTER-RECORD
        ADD 1 TO MASTER-OUT-COUNT.
IF (MASTER-SAVE-FLAG = "Y")
   THEN MOVE SAVE-AREA TO MASTER-RECORD
   ELSE PERFORM B00-GET-NEXT-MASTER-RECORD.
**** EXIT
```

A10-TRANS-KEY-LOW.
    [Here to process transactions less than master]
    IF (TRANS-ACTION = ADD-ACTION)
        THEN MOVE MASTER-RECORD TO SAVE-AREA
            MOVE TRANS-RECORD TO MASTER-RECORD
            MOVE "Y" TO MASTER-SAVE-FLAG
        ELSE error—delete or change to record not there; transaction ignored
            ADD 1 TO TRANS-ERROR-COUNT.
    PERFORM C00-GET-NEXT-TRANSACTION.
**** EXIT
A20-TRANS-EQUAL-MASTER.
    [Here to apply all transactions to master record]
    IF (TRANS-ACTION = CHANGE-ACTION)
        THEN IF (MASTER-DELETED-FLAG = "N")
            THEN MOVE TRANS-FIELDS TO MASTER-FIELDS
            ELSE error—changing deleted record; transaction ignored
                ADD 1 TO TRANS-ERROR-COUNT.
    IF (TRANS-ACTION = DELETE-ACTION)
        THEN IF (MASTER-DELETED-FLAG = "N")
            THEN MOVE "Y" TO MASTER-DELETED-FLAG
            ELSE error—deleting deleted record; transaction ignored
                ADD 1 TO TRANS-ERROR-COUNT.
    IF (TRANS-ACTION = ADD-ACTION)
        THEN IF (MASTER-DELETED-FLAG = "Y")
            THEN MOVE TRANS-RECORD TO MASTER-RECORD
                MOVE "N" TO MASTER-DELETED-FLAG
            ELSE error—adding record already there; transaction ignored
                ADD 1 TO TRANS-ERROR-COUNT.
    PERFORM C00-GET-NEXT-TRANSACTION.
**** EXIT
**** END OF A00-UPDATE-MASTER
B00-GET-NEXT-MASTER-RECORD.
    [Here to get a master record and check sequence and for duplicates]
    READ OLD-MASTER INTO MASTER-RECORD
        AT END MOVE HIGH-VALUES TO MASTER-KEY.
    IF (MASTER-KEY NOT = HIGH-VALUES)
        THEN ADD 1 TO MASTER-IN-COUNT.
    IF (MASTER-KEY < PREVIOUS-MASTER-KEY)
        THEN error—master file out of sequence; abort run
            GO TO Z90-STOP-RUN.
    IF (MASTER-KEY = PREVIOUS-MASTER-KEY)
        THEN error—duplicate master file record; record retained in new master
                                    file.
        [We abort the run if the master file is out of sequence; duplicate master file rec-
        ords are in error but won't affect the processing]
    MOVE MASTER-KEY TO PREVIOUS-MASTER-KEY.
**** END OF B00-GET-NEXT-MASTER-RECORD

C00-GET-NEXT-TRANSACTION.
  [Here to get a transaction, check its sequence, and check for illegal duplicates; notice
  that this takes almost as much code as the remainder of the update]
  MOVE "N" TO GOOD-TRANSACTION-FLAG.
  [Flag used to tell when we get a good transaction]
  PERFORM C10-GET-NEXT-GOOD-TRANSACTION
          UNTIL (GOOD-TRANSACTION-FLAG = "Y")
**** EXIT
C10-GET-NEXT-GOOD-TRANSACTION.
  READ TRANS-FILE INTO TRANS-RECORD
          AT END MOVE HIGH-VALUES TO TRANS-KEY.
  IF (TRANS-KEY NOT = HIGH-VALUES)
      THEN ADD 1 TO TRANS-COUNT.
  MOVE "Y" TO GOOD-TRANSACTION-FLAG.
  [Will reset if transaction contains an error]
  IF (TRANS-KEY NOT = HIGH-VALUES)
      THEN PERFORM C20-VALIDATE-TRANSACTIONS.
**** EXIT
C20-VALIDATE-TRANSACTIONS.
  IF (TRANS-KEY < PREVIOUS-TRANS-KEY)
      THEN error—transactions out of sequence; abort run
          GO TO Z90-STOP-RUN.
  IF ((TRANS-KEY = PREVIOUS-TRANS-KEY) AND
      (TRANS-ACTION < PREVIOUS-TRANS-ACTION))
      THEN error—transactions out of sequence; abort run
          GO TO Z90-STOP-RUN.
  IF (TRANS-ACTION = ADD-ACTION) OR
      (TRANS-ACTION = CHANGE-ACTION) OR
      (TRANS-ACTION = DELETE-ACTION)
      THEN NEXT SENTENCE
      ELSE error—invalid action code in transaction; transaction ignored
          MOVE "N" TO GOOD-TRANSACTION-FLAG.
  MOVE TRANS-KEY TO PREVIOUS-TRANS-KEY.
  MOVE TRANS-ACTION TO PREVIOUS-TRANS-ACTION.
  IF (GOOD-TRANSACTION-FLAG = "N")
      THEN ADD 1 TO TRANS-ERROR-COUNT.
**** EXIT
**** END OF C00-GET-NEXT-TRANSACTION

SEVEN

Random-Access Files

Random-access files are named for their ability to access records randomly. The term "random" is a little misleading since it makes it seem as if a READ results in a record being retrieved at random. In fact, you tell the system which record you want, and the system retrieves it directly. The term "random" comes about because the record being retrieved does not depend on the last record retrieved as it does with sequential access.

With sequential access, processing is like dealing cards from a card deck. To retrieve a specific card, you must deal the cards, one at a time, until you get the card you want. Random access is like spreading the cards out on the table, face up. To retrieve a specific card, you pick it up directly.

Random access is more efficient than sequential access where relatively few records are retrieved in a file, or where the transactions cannot be placed in the sort order of the file being accessed. Both reasons apply in many on-line systems. For a retrieval system, such as that used by a branch bank to check your account balance when you cash a check, a single transaction is applied to a large master file. It is not just the efficiency of random access, but often the response time that is important. Bank lines are long enough without having to wait to process the entire file sequentially to retrieve your account balance. As with many retrieval systems, the transactions are in random order. Banks have had little success in getting people to queue up in account number order, and this is not necessary with random access.

For random access, files must be stored on direct-access storage devices (also termed mass storage in COBOL). Random access does not preclude sequential processing. Records can be read sequentially from a random-access file, or they can be written sequentially into a random-access file to create the file. Sequential access is often used to create random-access files, and also to back up and restore them on sequential I/O devices such as tape.

There are three types of random access files: relative, direct, and indexed. A *relative* file is one in which the records are numbered sequentially. The key of the record is a sequential number that specifies the record's relative position within the file, analogous to the subscript of a table. In *direct* files the key has two components, a relative track number and a record key. The relative track number (track key) tells where the record is stored on the direct-access device. The record key identifies the record on the track. The system retrieves records randomly by locating the track containing the record, and then searching the records on the track for one with a matching key. For *indexed* files a portion of the file is set aside to contain a directory that tells on which track the records are stored. The system retrieves records randomly by first searching the directory, termed the index area, to find on which track the record is stored. It then goes to that track and searches it for a record with a missing key.

Relative and direct files, because they go to the track immediately without having to search an index, are faster for random access. Indexed files, because the system maintains an index of where the records are stored rather than requiring you to supply this information, are easier to use. Also, the separate index for indexed files makes it possible to expand the file when records are added.

Relative and direct files must be written in their entirety when they are created, and records cannot be added thereafter, although space can be reserved with dummy records. You supply the operating system with the key, as each record is written. To retrieve a record, you supply this same key. As an example, suppose that a personnel record for SMITH is written as the hundredth record and ends up on the tenth track of the file. For a relative file you would specify a key of 100 to retrieve the record. For a direct file you supply the track key of 10 and the name "SMITH" to retrieve the record. Relative and direct files are inconvenient because you must somehow derive the key to access a given record. They are also relatively inefficient for sequential processing because the records cannot be blocked.

To retrieve the record for SMITH with an indexed file, you simply supply SMITH as the record key and let the system search the index to find the track on which the record is stored. Indexed files do not need to be written in their entirety when they are created. New records can be added later.

Relative, direct, and indexed files can be updated in place. That is, individual records can be added, deleted, or changed without disturbing other records in the file. Updating records in place simplifies the updating logic, but leads to a serious backup problem. When a file is updated in place, the original version of the file is changed, and if the job must be rerun, the file must first be restored from a backup copy, presuming that one has been made. Sequential files do not have this problem because the original version of the file is not changed when it is updated, and it can be used to rerun the job if necessary. Thus while it is easy to update direct-access files, you must give more thought to backing them up. The usual technique is to back up the entire file at some point and save all subsequent transactions.

Although random-access files can be processed sequentially, they are less efficient than sequential files for this. Do not use random-access files unless you need to. As an alternative to direct or indexed files, a small sequential file can be read into an internal table so that the records can be retrieved using a sequential or binary search. (Records in a relative file could be subscripted directly in an internal table.)

The decision of whether to make a file sequential or random is generally straightforward because the two access methods are functionally different, and the functional needs will dictate which should be used. Selecting which of the three types of random access to use is more difficult because the differences are more in hardware implementation than in function. However, in practice the indexed random-access method is almost always used because of its greater power.

RELATIVE FILES

Relative files are analogous to tables. They are used when records can be easily associated with ascending, consecutive numbers. Their advantage over tables is that their size is limited by the amount of direct-access storage space rather than the more limited memory. However, it is much slower to retrieve a record from a relative file than it is from a table.

The disk space allocated to a relative file is formatted when the file is created, and additional space cannot be added thereafter. But records can be replaced, and so dummy records are often inserted to be replaced later with real records, which gives the same effect as adding records. Once a relative file is created, it can be updated by writing new records over the top of old ones.

Relative files must contain fixed-length records. You supply the relative record number as the key to read or write records. Since the key is the record's relative position in the file, the system does not store it as a part of the record. The system locates records by computing the track and the location of the record on the track from the record length, the length of a track, and the record's relative position in the file. Figure 8 illustrates a relative file.

If the records being stored in a relative file cannot be easily associated with ascending, consecutive numbers, such as for a personnel file, the record key, which might be the social security number, can be stored in a table along with the relative record number. The records would be written consecutively into the relative file, and the record key and relative record number stored as elements in the table. Thereafter, record retrieval based on the social security number would require two steps. First, the table would

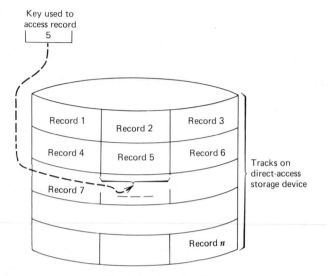

Figure 8 Relative file.

be searched to find the element with a matching social security number to obtain the relative record number. The relative record number would then be used to retrieve the record in the relative file. Figure 9 illustrates this method.

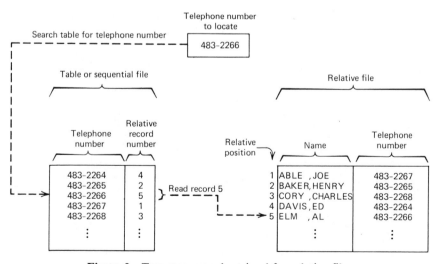

Figure 9 Two-step record retrieval for relative file.

The table could either be stored as a sequential file that is read into the table when records are to be retrieved from the relative file, or it could be made a relative file itself. Either way increases the effort required to access the file, and you might instead consider using a direct or indexed file.

DIRECT FILES

Direct files are used when records must be accessed in random order and new records are seldom added. Like relative files, the disk space allocated to the file is formatted when a direct file is created, and additional space cannot be added thereafter. Dummy records can be inserted to be replaced later with real records, giving the effect of adding records. Direct files are updated by writing new records over the top of old ones.

Direct files have two-part keys: a track key and a record key. The track key specifies the relative track in the file. The record key contains data to identify the record on the track. Several records may be stored on a track. To retrieve a record randomly, you supply both the track key and the record key. The system goes to the specified track and searches it for a record with the specified record key. Figure 10 illustrates a direct file.

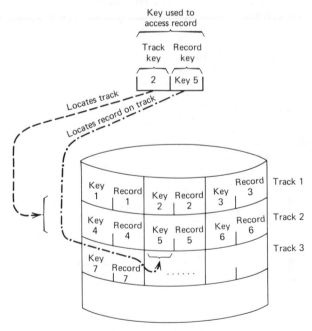

Figure 10   Direct file.

The difficulty with direct files is deriving the track key. The record key often comes from the record itself, and for a personnel file it might be a social security number. There are two ways to derive the track key. First, you can let COBOL supply the track key as it writes the records. But then you must save this track key, along with the record key, in a separate table or file. To retrieve a record, you would use the record key to search the table or file to find the track key. This is both complicated and inefficient. A better way is to compute the track keys from the record keys and supply them to COBOL when the records are written.

The remaindering method used for hash tables works well for this and is simple. Divide the record key by the largest prime number less than the number of tracks allocated, and use the remainder for the relative track number. If a prime number table is not available, use the largest odd number not ending in 5 that is less than the number of allocated tracks.

For an example, suppose that we have a personnel file containing 8000 employees in which 10 records will fit on a single track. The file requires 800 tracks, but we should allocate more to allow for growth, perhaps 1000 tracks. Also, the efficiency begins to drop off when the file becomes more than 70% full. To compute the relative track number, divide the social security number by 999, the largest odd number not ending in 5 that is less than 1000. A social security number of 520-44-1461 divided by 999 yields a remainder of 423, which becomes the relative track number. The remaindering method is described in more detail in Chapter 9 for hash tables.

INDEXED FILES

The record keys in indexed files are a part of the record. Each record must have a unique record key, and the records are stored in the file in ascending order, based on this key. For example, a personnel file might have the person's name as the record key. The file could be read sequentially to process the records for each person in the file, one at a time, in alphabetical order. Records can also be accessed randomly by specifying the record key so that the record for SMITH could be read by presenting SMITH as the record key. The file can also be positioned to any record in the file to begin sequential processing. Thus you could position the file to the record for SMITH, and sequentially read all the records that follow.

Indexed files contain both the records being stored and an index to the records. The index contains the record keys and the pointer to where the records are stored. The system automatically updates the index when records are added or deleted, and except for the JCL required to create the file, it is transparent to the user. Figure 11 illustrates a simplified file.

A major advantage of indexed files is that records can be added or de-

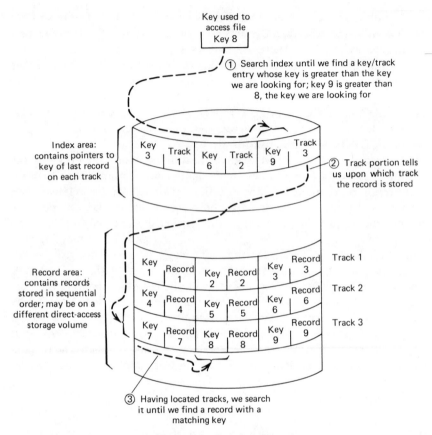

Figure 11   Indexed file.

leted. With sequential files, records can be added or deleted only by rewriting the entire file. Records cannot be added to relative or direct files unless dummy records have been inserted to allow room. Indexed files are slower to read sequentially than sequential files, and slower to read randomly than relative or direct files. How much slower depends on the implementation, but in the past the processing speed has been relatively slow.

As with sequential files, blocking for indexed files reduces the number of interblock gaps, conserving direct-access storage. Unlike sequential files, blocking for indexed files does not necessarily increase the I/O efficiency. It does when the file is processed sequentially, but not when it is processed randomly. For random access it is less efficient to bring in an entire block of records rather than just one unblocked record. Because the access is random, it is unlikely that the next record to be accessed would be in the same block as the last record brought in.

Indexed files are created by writing records into them sequentially. The system stores the records in blocks and maintains a separate index containing the key of the last record written in each block. The system retrieves records randomly by searching the index to find the block containing the record, and then searching the block for a record with a matching key. Indexed files can also be updated by replacing, adding, or deleting records. Records are replaced by overwriting the old record.

When indexed files are updated, the records are written into the file and the pointers are updated. If the program abnormally terminates during this process, the file may become unusable because the pointers may not get updated. This is a serious problem that requires you to back up the file at some point and save all the transactions entered thereafter until a new backup is made.

UPDATING RANDOM-ACCESS FILES

To update a random-access master file, a sequential transactions file is read and applied directly to the master file. The pseudocode for updating a random-access master file with a file of sequential transactions would be as follows:

Read trans-file into trans-record.
Do while no eof trans-file.
    If add
        then write master-record from trans-record
                    invalid key—error in adding a record already in file
    Else if delete
        then delete master-record
                    invalid key—error in record not found to delete
    Else if change
        then read master-file into master-record
                    invalid key—error in record not found to change
            move trans-record values to master-record
            write master-file from master-record.
    Read trans-file into trans-record.
    End.

Notice that since each transaction updates the master file as it is processed, no special logic is needed to handle several transactions being applied to the same master file record or a change transaction being applied to a previous add transaction.

EIGHT

Data Base Systems

Sooner or later you will come into contact with data base systems. A data base is a collection of related files. Since they are large and complex, you probably will not start your career by designing them. In fact, designing data base systems can become an entire career. But if your company has a data base system, you may write applications that retrieve information from the data base, or you may write programs to add new information.

THE NEED FOR DATA BASE SYSTEMS

Applications within companies tended to grow ad hoc, with separate master files generated for each new application. Inevitably the same information began to appear in several files. Not only did this waste storage, but more importantly, it made updating the information difficult because it had to be done separately for each file in which the information appeared. The files had separate programs updating and retrieving information from them so that a change in a data item or the addition of new information became a major programming task. Likewise, a hardware change could require extensive reprogramming of application programs.

Since many files grew up, some reports had to gather the information from several files. But the files were often generated with different programming languages, and could not be accessed by other languages. The information in several files was usually related in some way, such as employees working on projects, but the files had no way of representing the relationships. With the redundant data and with many people updating the files, the accuracy and the consistency of the data were suspect.

Controlling access to sensitive information in the files became unmanageable. Not everyone can be allowed to change the payroll file, for example, as this might be a little hard on cash flow. And not everyone should be permitted access to every field in a file. Companies do not want employees perusing a payroll file to find out everyone's salary.

A further problem companies had was providing access to the data. Sometimes duplicate files were generated because people did not know that the data they needed already existed in another file. The same data was often needed by groups in different locations. Some users needed only slow batch access, while others required immediate on-line response. Consequently the data storage problem encompassed a data communications problem.

THE PURPOSE OF DATA BASE SYSTEMS

Data base systems grew out of these needs, and they also came about because companies recognized the value of information about themselves and their operations. The data base allowed people to think about the data needs of the entire company and how they were interrelated. They began to recognize that they had to treat information as a valuable commodity.

Data base systems solved the problems in several ways. The problems of redundancy were solved by having a coherent overview of the data, knowing where it appeared, and having a single entry point that updated the data wherever it appeared. Some data bases stored the information only once, placing pointers to the data wherever else it logically appeared. The end result was to make the data consistent.

Since the data base was designed coherently, it could have consistent data storage and organization, which permitted standard access to the data. There was only one data base with a standard update and retrieval language.

The data base systems allowed a wide range of applications in using the data. Centralizing the data made it easier for diverse users to access the data because the data was better documented and better publicized. It also permitted the application programs to access the information in the manner they needed. One application might treat the data base as a sequential file and another as a random file. Different applications might access the same records in the data base using different data elements as the record key. For example, the personnel file could be used to locate the department of an individual. Another application could use the same file to locate all the employees in a department.

Data base systems were given elaborate data structures to show the relationship of data. The data might be stored in several physical files, with the data structure representing the relationship between data in the different files. An application program might retrieve a logical record in which, unknown to it, data elements are stored in separate physical files.

In order to control access to the data and ensure its security, two things were necessary. First, the software was given the facility for limiting access to specific fields. Second, companies provided organizational control of the data base. A person or group was given full authority and responsibility for the data base, including organization, access, and backup. This position was termed the *data base administrator*.

Data base systems also uncoupled the logical data, the data as we use it, from the physical data, the data as it is physically stored. This way, if the hardware changed, if an improved access method was installed, or if attributes were added or removed from records, the application programs accessing the file did not need to be changed. For example, an application accessing the personnel file to obtain an employee's name and job title would not need to be changed if other fields were added to or deleted from the personnel file.

The application program did not need to know the format of the data; the data base system could convert it to the desired format as necessary. Nor did the application program need to know the characteristics of the I/O device upon which the data base was stored or how the data was physically organized on the device. In essence, the application program could tell the data base system what it wanted done, and let the data base system worry about how to do it.

Today, data base systems are in wide use, but they are not without their problems. They required a great deal of effort to design, maintain, control, and use. Programming a data base system is difficult and usually requires learning one or more new programming languages. Efficiency can be a problem because the versatility of the data base system is often at the expense of efficiency.

But the main problems of data base systems are the eternal problems of centralization versus decentralization. Centralizing gives better overall control, makes things more consistent, makes things easier to share, and can do efficiently what is intended to be done. However, centralizing makes things vulnerable because everything is in one place. Centralized systems are usually not responsive to the needs of particular groups, and they are difficult to change. It may be impossible to do something other than what the centralized system was intended to do.

By contrast, decentralized systems are often responsive to particular groups, are less vulnerable to a single catastrophy, and may be relatively easy to change. Their disadvantage is that usually there is redundant effort. Each location may do things differently so that it is difficult to merge or share things.

And so there are advantages and disadvantages to data base systems. They represent the culmination of the centralization of information in an organization. However, centralization and decentralization go in cycles, and so we can expect to see decentralization of data emphasized in the next cyclical swing. Already some data bases are distributed to several processors for storage and maintenance. Today this is done for hardware efficiency, but soon it may be done to give particular groups more control over their own data.

PROGRAMMING DATA BASE SYSTEMS

Data bases do not come easy. Although they are a logical extension of file systems, they required a quantum lead in software support. Data base systems are inherently large and complex. It is almost impossible to write an entire data base system in COBOL. Instead, a separate data base language is needed; in fact, several languages.

A language is needed to describe the overall data base. This language, termed the schema description language, is used by the data base administrator. The *schema* is a description of the logical data base, which is the data base as it appears to the user. The schema identifies not only the records (entities and their attributes), but also the relationship of one to another. For example, it might describe separate records representing both the departments within a company and the employees. Not only would the schema allow us to specify the organizational hierarchy, but also to show the assignment of employees to departments.

The schema describes the overall data base, but the data base also needs to be accessed by application programs. Perhaps an application program wants to generate an employee listing. For this, the subschema description language was developed. The *subschema* is a description of a part of the data base needed by a particular application. It allows application programs to deal with the data base as if it contained only the data in which they are interested.

Both the schema and the subschema description languages deal with the logical data base. Yet another language is required to deal with the physical data base. The data description language does this. It knows how the data is stored, the hardware upon which it is stored, and how to physically access the data.

Next is a data manipulation language. The data manipulation language retrieves and updates the data base, and is used by application programs, usually through subroutine calls.

There is, of course, the application programming language, such as COBOL. The application program uses the subschema language to describe the portion of the data base it needs, and then uses the data manipulation language to access the data.

In addition to these languages, there may be high-level query languages for perusing data in the data base, and there will usually be a language to provide the communications facilities needed to allow remote users to access the data base.

DATA BASE ADMINISTRATOR

The heart of the data base system is not the data, but a person or group, the data base administrator. The data base administrator provides centralized control of the data and coordinates its use. The data base administrator also restricts access to the data base, allowing only authorized persons to access each field in the data. The data base administrator publicizes the data and tells how it may be accessed. Data bases are tightly controlled, and a great deal of formality is required. Because the data base serves a wide range of users, the documentation of the data becomes extremely important. Each data element described in the data dictionary may require more documentation than an entire file in a simple application.

The data base administrator is responsible for backing up the data base and for recovering it when required. With a large, central data base used by many applications, a company could be put out of business if it lost its data base. The data base administrator also reorganizes the data base as necessary to keep it efficient. The data base administrator may periodically audit the data base to ensure that errors have not crept in, and monitor the use and performance of the data base.

DATA STRUCTURES

In order to show the relationship of data, various data structures were developed. Generally there are two ways to show relationship. The first is physical proximity. In a record, all the data items in the record are known to be attributes of the same entity because they are all stored in the same record. If a record in a file represented a person, the record might contain the name of children as attributes. Since there might be several children, the record would be of variable length, with a segment for each child. These repeating segments, sometimes termed repeating groups, are a common way of showing relationship by physical proximity.

List Structure

The second way to show relationship is with pointers. The simple list structure shown in Figure 12 illustrates a pointer system. If we retrieve any record in the list, we can find all the records in the list that logically follow it.

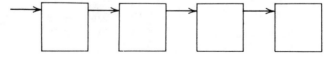

Figure 12   List structure.

To add a record to the list, we do not physically move it; we simply change the pointers. With pointers, the order in which the records are physically stored does not determine their order; the pointers do this.

Ring structure

The ring structure is similar to the list, except that the last record points back to the first, as shown in Figure 13. This way when we retrieve a record, we can find all other records by searching forward.

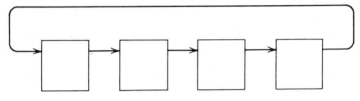

Figure 13 Ring structure.

A further level of sophistication is to have both forward and backward pointers. This gives immediate access to the records on either side of a record, and it simplifies the insertion and deletion of records because we have immediate access to the records whose pointers need changing.

Inverted List Structure

The inverted list structure arranges attributes of a record in sort order by providing pointers for the attributes. The concept is actually very simple. Suppose that our list structure represented a telephone book containing names and telephone numbers. To place the entries in order by name, the list structure would have pointers from one record to the next, in the order of the names. If we invert the file on the telephone number, this means we order the file on the telephone number. In a sequential file we would sort on the telephone number, but this destroys the order of the file on name. In a list structure we would leave the order on name intact, and add a pointer in each entry to point from one telephone number to the next, in the order of the telephone numbers. Figure 14 represents this.

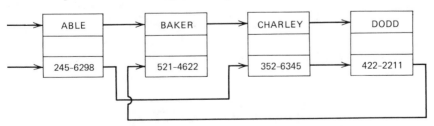

Figure 14 Inverted list structure.

Hierarchy Structure

By using a combination of the data structures, we come to the hierarchy or tree structure. Each element in the structure is a node. It can have one owner, but may have several members. Figure 15 illustrates a hierarchy. Notice that a hierarchy may contain redundant data. Data base systems such as IBM's IMS are based on the hierarchy.

The hierarchy is searched from top to bottom and from left to right. To find all the children of parent 2, we would look at each grandparent, and then at the parents owned by the grandparent, until we found each occurrence of parent 2. Then we would look at all the children of each parent 2 occurrence. To find all the parents of child 3, we would search the hierarchy from top to bottom to locate every child, and note the parent of each instance of child 3.

Network Structure

The next data structure is the network, which is obtained by removing some of the restrictions of the hierarchy. An element can have several owners, in addition to owning several members. An element can own other elements several levels down. Pointers can point upwards as well as downwards. Searching a network becomes complex. In fact, you do more than search— you navigate. Figure 16 shows a network. It is the same structure as shown in Figure 15, but note that the pointers eliminate the redundant data of P2 and C3. The CODASYL DBTG is based on the network.

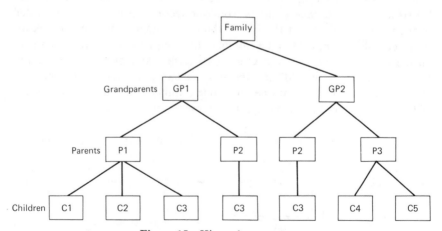

Figure 15   Hierarchy structure.

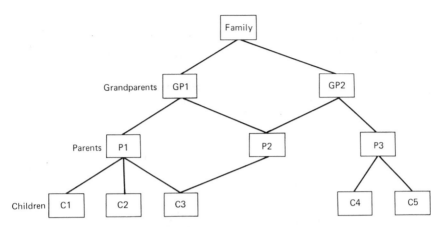

Figure 16 Network structure.

If we wanted to find the children of parent 2, the search would be the same as for the hierarchy, except that there would be only one occurrence of P2. If we wanted to find the parents of child 3, we would search the network for child 3, and then child 3 would point to all its parents.

Inverted Hierarchy or Network

Yet another structure is the inverted hierarchy or network. The structure is a hierarchy or network, but it is then inverted on specified attributes. If we have a hierarchy representing a family, we could invert on the age of the children so that we could quickly locate all children of a given age. Inverted data base systems are represented by System 2000, ADABASE, META-BASE, and TOTAL.

Relational Data Base

The final popular data structure is the relational model. The relational data organization is very simple in concept, but difficult to implement. To date there have been few successful implementations, mainly because of performance problems, but the lure of the relational model is such that it is predicted to become the most popular data base system in the future. Part of the allure is that the relational data model is based on the mathematical theory of relations, and it can be accessed using relational algebra and relational calculus. Who could resist this?

Because relational data bases are based on mathematics, the terminology is different. Records are termed *tuples*, a file is termed a *relation*, and a field is termed a *domain*. All of this obscures the basic simplicity of the relational approach.

In the relational model the data is represented as a table, where each row is a record (or tuple), each column is a field (or domain), and the table is the file (or relation). By placing the previous family into the relational form as a table, it would appear as follows:

Grandparent	Parent	Child
GP1	P1	C1
GP1	P1	C2
GP1	P1	C3
GP1	P2	C3
GP2	P2	C3
GP2	P3	C4
GP2	P3	C5

To find all the children of P1, we look in the parent column for each occurrence of P1, and the children appear in the child column. To find the parents of C3, we look in the child column for all occurrences of C3, and the parents appear in the parent column.

These brief paragraphs only introduce the data base concepts. A full understanding of even one data base system would require an entire book.

NINE

Tables

Tables have two important purposes in programs. They reduce the amount of code that must be written, and they make programs more flexible by allowing related items to be parameterized. For example, suppose that you need to expand the post office abbreviations for states into their full names, such as deriving CALIFORNIA from CA. One way to do this would be the following:

```
IF STATE-CODE = "AL"
   THEN MOVE "ALABAMA" TO STATE-NAME
ELSE IF STATE-CODE = "AK"
   THEN MOVE "ARKANSAS" TO STATE-NAME
ELSE . . .
ELSE IF STATE-CODE = "WY"
   THEN MOVE "WYOMING" TO STATE-NAME.
```

You would undoubtedly incur an acute case of writer's cramp before you reached Nevada, and complete tetany as you inch toward Rhode Island. Instead, you could define a table to contain the abbreviations and state names, and search the table to find the matching abbreviation.

```
01  STATES-TABLE.
    05  STATES OCCURS 50 TIMES INDEXED BY STATE-NO.
        10  STATE-CODE        PIC X(2).
        10  STATE-NAME        PIC X(14).
```

Ignoring for the present the problem of how we get the values into the table, the COBOL SEARCH verb can now find an entry in the table as follows:

```
SET STATE-NO TO 1.
SEARCH STATES-TABLE
    AT END error—state code not found
    WHEN abbreviation = STATE-CODE (STATE-NO) abbreviation
                                        found in table.
```

Besides saving program statements, tables minimize the impact of change. If a state is added or deleted, we simply change the table. The coding within the program need not change at all. If data items change within the table, again the coding need not be changed. For example, if the spelling of states were to be put on a more rational basis so that it corresponds to the way the names are pronounced, such as changing Arkansas to Arkansaw and Illinois to Illinoy, the changes could all be accomplished in the table without changing the code at all. This is important because when you make changes to the code within a program, there is a chance for error.

Tables can be filled either by assigning them initial values or by reading them in from a file. COBOL does not allow tables to be assigned initial values directly. You must code the data items individually and then redefine them as a table.

```
01   STATES-TABLE-VALUES.
     05   ARKANSAS-CODE     PIC X(2) VALUE "AK".
     05   ARKANSAS-NAME     PIC X(14) VALUE "ARKANSAS".
            .
            .
            .
     05   WYOMING-NAME      PIC X(14) VALUE "WYOMING".
01   STATES-TABLE REDEFINES STATES-TABLE-VALUES.
     05   STATES OCCURS 50 TIMES INDEXED BY STATE-NO.
          10   STATE-CODE   PIC X(2).
          10   STATE-NAME   PIC X(14).
```

The other way of filling a table, reading in values from a file, is described in a following section. If the values seldom change, build them into the table. If the values change with any frequency, read them in from a file. The file is usually a card deck, which is easily changed. If the size of the table will change, store the current table size as a data item, assigning it an initial value so that the table size is also a parameter.

Tables are one of the most important tools at your disposal to simplify writing and changing programs. Make yourself so familiar with tables that their use and coding become automatic.

TYPES OF TABLES

There are four usual types of tables: direct, sequential, binary, and hash.

Direct Tables

A direct table is indexed rather than searched. If a month were entered in the form mm, and the number of days in a month were contained in a table with an entry for each month, the numeric month mm could be used to index the table directly to find the number of days in a month.

Sequential Tables

A sequential table is searched consecutively from beginning to end, if necessary, to find the table entry. Since the table is searched in its entirety, it need be in no particular order. Assuming a full table with random distribution, it requires an average of $n/2$ searches to find a given entry in a table of size n. If the item is not in the table, it will always take n searches. It is more efficient to place at the beginning of the table the items most likely to be accessed. In a table containing state names, you should place California and New York at the front, and Wyoming and Alaska at the end. The COBOL SEARCH verb is a convenient way of searching sequential tables. It is so simple to use that it needs little explanation.

SET index TO entry-with-which-to-start.
SEARCH table
    AT END imparative-statement-for-entry-not-found
    WHEN condition imparative-statement-for-entry-FOUND
      .
      .
      .
    WHEN condition imparative-statement-for-entry-found.

Binary Tables

A binary table must be arranged in ascending or descending order on the key—some data item within the table. The binary search begins in the middle of the table and continues to the middle of the lower or upper half of the table, depending on whether the current key was high or low. This continues until the element is found or the table is exhausted.

A binary search is more efficient for large tables than is a sequential search, although it requires the table to be in some sort order. To understand a binary search, suppose that we are trying to guess a number from 1 to 100, and the number is 64. With a sequential search we would guess 1, 2, 3, ..., 64, requiring a total of 64 guesses. With a binary search our first guess is 50 (too low), but now we know that the number must be in the range from 51 to 100. With the first guess we have cut the size of the table we need to search in half. Our next guess is halfway between 51 and 100, 74 (too high), 62 (too low), 68 (too high), 65 (too high), 63 (too low), and 64 (eureka).

The 64 is found with only seven guesses. Notice that with each guess we cut in half the size of the remaining table that must be searched. The larger the table, the more efficient the binary search becomes. For a table of size n, it requires on the order of $n \log_2 n$ searches for an item, even if the item is not found in the table. To locate the number 643 in a table of 1000 elements would require 643 sequential searches, but only nine binary searches.

A sequential search is slightly faster for small tables than a binary search. A binary search becomes more efficient than a sequential search when there are roughly 60 elements in the table, excluding the time it may take to place the table in sort order for the binary search. In general, use a binary search if the table is in ascending or descending order. If a large, unordered table is searched often, sort it and use a binary search.

The SEARCH ALL verb in COBOL does a binary search. For the binary search, the ASCENDING KEY or DESCENDING KEY clauses must be added to the table description.

```
05   table OCCURS n TIMES INDEXED BY index
            ASCENDING KEY IS table-entry
            DESCENDING KEY IS another-table-entry
            .
            .
            .
```

```
         □   □
SEARCH ALL table
    AT END imparative-statement-for-entry-not-found
    WHEN key = expression imperative-statement-for-entry-found.
```

If for some reason you must write your own binary search, the following pseudocode illustrates how it might be coded:

```
Set low-index to 1.
Set high-index to max-table-size.
Set found-index to zero.
Do while [(low-index ≤ high-index) and (found-index = zero)].
    temp = (low-index + high-index)/2.
    If table (temp) = key
        then found-index = temp
        else if table (temp) < key
                then low-index = temp + 1
                else high-index = temp - 1.
    End.
If found-index = zero.
    then error--table entry not found.
```

Hash Tables

Sometimes it is impractical to use a sequential or a binary search. Perhaps we must add to the table while it is being searched. We could still use a sequential search by adding new entries to the end of the table, or a binary search by finding where the new entry is to be added and moving all the elements from there on down one slot to make room. However, the sequential search or updating the table for a binary search may be too slow.

An alternative is to use a hash table. Rather than search the table for a key that matches, we compute a subscript into the table and use it instead. Let us take as an example a table used to retrieve a person's name, given the social security number. Let us also suppose that there are transactions to add new names. Assuming that there are 1000 names to store, we need a technique to convert the 9-digit social security numbers into numbers ranging from 1 to 1000.

The simplest method is to divide the social security numbers by 1000 and take the remainder, which will range in value from 0 to 999, and add 1 to it to bring it into the subscript range from 1 to 1000. The remainders are more evenly distributed if we divide by the largest prime number less than 1000. (A prime number is a number divisible only by 1 and itself, such as 7 and 11.) The largest prime number less than 1000 is 997. If you do not have access to a prime number table, select the largest odd number less than 1000 which does not end in 5. For our example, we shall use 999.

Now let us see how this works in practice. The number 520-44-1461 yields a remainder of 423 when divided by 999, and the number 520-44-1462 yields a remainder of 424. So far so good, but the number 558-56-0304 also yields a remainder of 423, the same as 520-44-1461. This raises the problem of collisions—when two numbers yield the same remainder. It means that we cannot use the subscript directly. Instead, we will use it as the location at which to begin looking for a place to store the entry. But first we must initialize the table, probably with blanks or zeros, so that we can tell if an element contains an entry. We should also increase the size of the table to provide room for the collisions, perhaps to 1500 elements, and then divide by 1499 to compute the subscripts. The larger the table, the less chance of collisions and the more efficient it becomes. The efficiency begins to drop off when the table becomes more than about 70% full.

There is still a problem at the end of the table. What if several social security numbers yield a subscript of 1500? This is solved by wrapping around to the beginning of the table. To retrieve an entry from the table, we compute the subscript from the social security number and use this as the location at which to begin looking for the social security number in the table.

To illustrate a hash table, let us use the social security example to add and retrieve a person's name from a table. We shall define the table and write procedures to add new entries to the table and search it. The table is described as follows:

```
01  SS-TABLE.
    05  SS-NAME              PIC X(25).
*                            NAME OF PERSON FOR STORING AND
*                                                RETRIEVAL.
    05  SS-NO                PIC S9(9).
*                            SOCIAL-SECURITY NUMBER FOR
*                                STORING AND RETRIEVAL.
    05  SS-DIV               PIC S9(9) COMP-3 VALUE 1499.
*                            LARGEST ODD NUMBER NOT ENDING
*                                IN 5 LESS THAN SS-MAX-SIZE.
    05  SS-TEMP              PIC S9(9) COMP-3.
*                            SCRATCH STORAGE TO STORE
*                                                DIVIDEND.
    05  SS-MAX-SIZE          PIC S9(4) COMP SYNC VALUE 1500.
*                            SIZE OF PERSON ARRAY.
    05  SS-SUBSCRIPT         PIC S9(9) COMP-3.
*                            COMPUTED SUBSCRIPT.
    05  SS-PERSON            OCCURS 1500 TIMES INDEXED BY IP.
        10  SS-PERSON-NO     PIC S9(9).
*                            SOCIAL SECURITY NUMBER.
        10  SS-PERSON-NAME   PIC X(25).
*                            NAME OF PERSON.
            □  □
[First zero out the PERSON array]
PERFORM A20-ZERO-PERSON
    VARYING SS-SUBSCRIPT FROM 1 BY 1
    UNTIL SS-SUBSCRIPT > SS-MAX-SIZE.
            □  □
A20-ZERO-PERSON.
    MOVE ZEROS TO SS-PERSON-NO (SS-SUBSCRIPT).
**** EXIT
```

Next we must write a procedure to add entries to the table. The person's name must first be moved to SS-NAME, and the social security number to SS-NO. The procedure is performed as follows:

```
MOVE social-security-number TO SS-NO.
MOVE person's-name TO SS-NAME.
PERFORM C10-ADD-NAME.
```

The procedure is written as follows.

**** PROCEDURE TO ADD ENTRIES TO PERSON TABLE.
C10-ADD-NAME.
      DIVIDE SS-NO BY SS-DIV GIVING SS-TEMP
         REMAINDER SS-SUBSCRIPT.
      ADD 1 TO SS-SUBSCRIPT.
      SET IP TO SS-SUBSCRIPT.
      SEARCH SS-PERSON
        AT END PERFORM C10-WRAP-AROUND
        WHEN SS-PERSON-NO (IP) = ZEROS
           MOVE SS-NO TO SS-PERSON-NO (IP)
           MOVE SS-NAME TO SS-PERSON-NAME (IP).
**** EXIT
C10-WRAP-AROUND.
      SET IP TO 1.
      SEARCH SS-PERSON
        WHEN IP = SS-SUBSCRIPT
          DISPLAY "ERROR--SS-PERSON TABLE FULL, RUN
                             TERMINATED."
          DISPLAY "INCREASE SS-PERSON, SS-DIV, SS-MAX-
                            SIZE AND RECOMPILE."
          GO TO Z90-STOP-RUN
        WHEN SS-PERSON-NO (IP) = ZEROS
          MOVE SS-NO TO SS-PERSON-NO (IP)
          MOVE SS-NAME TO SS-PERSON-NAME (IP).
**** EXIT
**** END OF C10-ADD-NAME

We also need a procedure to retrieve a person's name, given the social security number. The social security number is first moved to SS-NO, and the name is returned in SS-NAME. If the name is not found, SS-NAME contains spaces. The procedure is performed as follows:

MOVE social-security-number TO SS-NO.
PERFORM C20-RETRIEVE-NAME.

The procedure is written as follows.

```
**** PROCEDURE TO RETRIEVE A PERSON'S NAME.
C20-RETRIEVE-NAME.
      DIVIDE SS-NO BY SS-DIV GIVING SS-TEMP
        REMAINDER SS-SUBSCRIPT.
      ADD 1 TO SS-SUBSCRIPT.
      SET IP TO SS-SUBSCRIPT.
      SEARCH SS-PERSON
        AT END PERFORM A20-WRAP-AROUND
        WHEN SS-PERSON-NO (IP) = ZERO
          MOVE SPACES TO SS-NAME
        WHEN SS-NO = SS-PERSON-NO (IP)
          MOVE SS-PERSON-NAME (IP) TO SS-NAME.
**** EXIT
C20-WRAP-AROUND.
      SET IP TO 1.
      SEARCH SS-PERSON
        WHEN IP = SS-SUBSCRIPT
          MOVE SPACES TO SS-NAME
        WHEN SS-NO = SS-PERSON-NO (IP)
          MOVE SS-PERSON-NAME (IP) TO SS-NAME.
**** EXIT
**** END OF C20-RETRIEVE-NAME
```

The remaining problem is what to do if the key is alphanumeric rather than numeric. This is solved in many computers by moving the alphanumeric item to a computational data item. When moved to such an item, the zone bits are removed from the alphanumeric characters to yield only numeric digits. A to I becomes 1 to 9, J to R becomes 1 to 9, and S to Z becomes 2 to 9. The following example illustrates this. The person's name and not the social security number is used to compute the subscript:

```
05  SS-NAME             PIC X(25).
05  SS-SHORT-NAME REDEFINES SS-NAME PIC X(18).
          [Many computers allow only 18 digits for a numeric data item]
05  SS-CONVERT     PIC S9(18) COMP.
      □   □
MOVE SS-SHORT-NAME TO SS-CONVERT.
DIVIDE SS-CONVERT BY SS-DIV GIVING SS-TEMP
    REMAINDER SS-SUBSCRIPT.
```

Fortunately hash tables are seldom needed. For a table with few entries, a sequential search would be simpler and more efficient. If only a few entries are added to the table but it is searched often, we might use a binary search and move all the entries in the table down to make room for a new entry. The hash table technique is also used for direct-access I/O in which the entries are records stored in a direct file rather than being elements of a table in memory.

READING IN TABLES

Reading in a table from a file does not seem like such a big deal, and it is not if it is done correctly. But your first experience with an incorrect method might occur when an old production program terminates one day with a message reading "TABLE OVERFLOW". It may take several excruciating hours to locate which table overflowed, all the while giving status reports to an irate customer who keeps calling for the report. You might conclude that the only appropriate punishment for a programmer who gave a "TABLE OVERFLOW" message without naming the table in a program containing 12 tables would be burning telephone poles under the fingernails.

To illustrate a technique for reading values into a table, we shall read a personnel file and store the employee IDs in a table, perhaps to validate transactions with a binary search. There are several things to note in this example. First, the payroll file has 1000 byte records, but we will need to save only the 10-byte employee ID. The table is of variable size because the number of employees will change. If the table overflows or comes close to overflowing, a message is printed telling how to change the program. The payroll file must be sorted in ascending order on the employee ID, and the program checks to ensure that this has been done.

```
77  OLD-ID               PIC X(10).
*                        OLD-ID CHECKS THE SORT ORDER
*                                OF THE INPUT TABLE.
****  EMPLOYEE FILE. RECORD LENGTH = 1000.
01  EMPLOYEE.
    05  EMPLOYEE-ID.     PIC X(10).
    05  FILLER           PIC X(990).
****  TABLE OF EMPLOYEE IDS.
01  ID-RECORD.
    05  ID-MAX           PIC S9(4) COMP VALUE 1000.
*                        MAXIMUM NUMBER OF IDS IN TABLE.
    05  ID-NO            PIC S9(4) COMP VALUE ZERO.
*                        CURRENT SIZE OF TABLE.
```

```
    05  ID-TABLE           OCCURS 0 TO 1000 TIMES
                           DEPENDING ON ID-NO
                           INDEXED BY IDX
                           ASCENDING KEY IS ID-ID.
        10  ID-ID          PIC X(10).
            □   □
    OPEN INPUT PAY-IN.
    MOVE LOW-VALUES TO EMPLOYEE-ID,    [EMPLOYEE-ID is set to
                        OLD-ID.            HIGH-VALUES at end-of-
                                           file, and OLD-ID checks the
                                           sequence of the input file]
    PERFORM B20-STORE-IDS
        UNTIL EMPLOYEE-ID = HIGH-VALUES.
    IF ID-NO + 5 > ID-MAX
        THEN DISPLAY "NOTE--ID-TABLE ABOUT TO OVERFLOW."
            DISPLAY "INCREASE ID-MAX, ID-TABLE AND
                                        RECOMPILE."
            □   □
B20-STORE-IDS.
    READ PAY-IN INTO EMPLOYEE
        AT END MOVE HIGH-VALUES TO EMPLOYEE-ID.
    IF EMPLOYEE-ID NOT = HIGH-VALUES
        THEN PERFORM B20-PART-A.
**** EXIT
B20-PART-A.
    IF EMPLOYEE-ID < OLD-ID
        THEN DISPLAY "ERROR--PAYROLL FILE NOT IN SORT,
                                    RUN TERMINATED."
            DISPLAY "OLD ID:  ", OLD-ID, "  CURRENT ID:  ",
                                        EMPLOYEE-ID
            GO TO Z90-STOP-RUN.
    MOVE EMPLOYEE-ID TO OLD-ID.
    ADD 1 TO ID-NO.
    IF ID-NO > ID-MAX
        THEN DISPLAY "ERROR--ID-TABLE OVERFLOW, RUN
                                        TERMINATED."
            DISPLAY "PAYROLL RECORD:  ", EMPLOYEE-ID
            DISPLAY "INCREASE ID-MAX, ID-TABLE AND
                                        RECOMPILE."
            GO TO Z90-STOP-RUN.
    MOVE EMPLOYEE-ID TO ID-ID (ID-NO).
**** EXIT
**** END OF B20-STORE-ID
```

Now whenever an ID is to be validated, we can code the following:

```
SEARCH  ALL  ID-TABLE
    AT  END  statement-if-not-found
    WHEN  ID-ID  (IDX)  =  id
        statement-if-found.
```

An application program might validate table entries as they are read because they too can contain errors. If a table is used by several programs, such as a date table, you might write a program to read the table from cards, validate it, and write it onto direct-access storage. Then any programs using the table can read it from direct-access storage, knowing that it is already validated. In reading in the table, you may be able to compute some initial values rather than having them entered. A program reading in a date table from cards might compute the cumulative work days in the year rather than having this information entered on the cards. Table maintenance programs are an important part of a system.

TEN

Sorting

Sorting is omnipresent in business applications. Entire books have been written about sorting, but it is essentially a simple process and should not take much programming time.

DESIGNING A SORT

Sorting consists of arranging records in either ascending or descending order based upon one or more fields within the record. There may be several fields upon which to sort, and the order in which the fields are listed determines the order in which they are sorted. For example, if the first field upon which to sort is the state and the second the city, the records would first be sorted in order by state and then in order by city within state.

Records before sorting are:

ALABAMA   JACKSONVILLE
ARKANSAS   OZARK
ALABAMA   ALABASTER
CALIFORNIA   ANAHEIM
ARKANSAS   JACKSONVILLE
ALABAMA   ABBEVILLE
CALIFORNIA   BARSTOW

Records after sorting on state and city in ascending order are:

ALABAMA   ABBEVILLE
ALABAMA   ALABASTER
ALABAMA   JACKSONVILLE
ARKANSAS   JACKSONVILLE
ARKANSAS   OZARK
CALIFORNIA   ANAHEIM
CALIFORNIA   BARSTOW

Sorting the records on descending order reverses the sequence:

CALIFORNIA	BARSTOW
CALIFORNIA	ANAHEIM
ARKANSAS	OZARK
ARKANSAS	JACKSONVILLE
ALABAMA	JACKSONVILLE
ALABAMA	ALABASTER
ALABAMA	ABBEVILLE

Sorting on city in ascending order and then on state in descending order arranges the records in yet another way:

ALABAMA	ABBEVILLE
ALABAMA	ALABASTER
CALIFORNIA	ANAHEIM
CALIFORNIA	BARSTOW
ARKANSAS	JACKSONVILLE
ALABAMA	JACKSONVILLE
ARKANSAS	OZARK

There are two common collating sequences that determine the sort order, the EBCDIC sequence and the ASCII sequence. EBCDIC has the following collating sequence from low to high:

blank
. < (+ $ *) ; - / , > ' = "
A through Z
0 through 9

The ASCII collating sequence from low to high differs:

blank
" $ ' ( ) * + , - . /
0 through 9
; < = >
A through Z

Although sorting is usually straightforward, nothing is ever without its complications. Sometimes exceptions are needed in the sort sequence such as sorting the name O'NEIL as if it were spelled ONEIL. Library systems in which books are sorted by title are incredibly difficult. The convention is for articles such as "the" to be omitted from the sort unless they are part of a proper noun, as for example "The Hague" or "Los Angeles" (the sort must handle foreign words too). Numbers are sorted as if they were spelled out (the number 12 would sort as if it were written twelve), and abbreviations are also sorted as if they were spelled out.

Although most sort utilities provide exits to enable you to go in and modify a record before it is sorted, the only practical way of handling such complications is to carry a separate sort field in the record to allow the field to be entered exactly as it is to be sorted. Although this requires entering the data twice, once as it actually is and once as it is to be sorted, it allows you to sort the records as you want, without spending your career writing the complex logic to handle the sorting exceptions.

Another problem occurs in files containing more than one record type. The fields to be sorted may be in different positions in different record types. For example, records such as the following may need to be sorted. Record type 1 contains names and states. Record type 2 contains city, state, and population of the city.

01	JONES			TEXAS	
01	SMITH			ARKANSAS	
02		CLEVELAND	OHIO		800476	
01	WILSON			WASHINGTON	
02		CHICAGO	ILLINOIS		4702000	

Suppose that we want to sort the records on state and then record type 1 on name and record type 2 on population. We can do that by appending a sort key. We must enlarge the record to contain a sort key and move the data items upon which to sort into the sort key so that both records will sort in the proper sequence. In the following records, sorting on the entire sort key in ascending order will sort record type 1 on state and name in ascending order and record type 2 on state and population in ascending order.

Sort Key

01	TEXAS	JONES	JONES		TEXAS	
01	ARKANSAS	SMITH	SMITH		ARKANSAS	
02	OHIO	800476		CLEVELAND	OHIO		800476	
01	WASHINGTON	WILSON	WILSON		WASHINGTON	
02	ILLINOIS	4702000		CHICAGO	ILLINOIS		4702000	

There are two ways to sort random-access files. One way is to sort the random-access files as you would a sequential file. However, some sort utilities will not accept a random-access file as input, requiring that you first copy it into a sequential file.

Another way to sort a random-access file is to use a tag sort. In a tag sort, the record key and the data fields upon which to sort are stripped from the records and sorted by themselves. Then the sorted keys are used to retrieve the random-access records in the new sort order. This technique is often used in on-line applications where fast response is required.

MEANS OF SORTING

There are three usual ways of sorting files: with the operating system sort utility, with the sort facility provided by the programming language such as the COBOL SORT verb, or by coding the sort yourself.

System Sort Utility

Your first choice for a sort should be the system sort utility. It is easier to code than to write all the necessary COBOL statements. It isolates the sort in a separate job step, which can minimize rerun time and help isolate errors. It reduces the maximum memory requirements because the sort program does not reside in memory with a COBOL program. It even simplifies maintenance because a sort utility can be changed without changing and recompiling a COBOL program.

The sort utilities differ with each operating system, but generally they consist of some JCL to specify the input and output files, and a sort statement in which you list the fields in the order in which you want to sort. For each field you give the starting byte position, the number of bytes in the field, the format of the field (binary, packed decimal, alphanumeric, etc.), and whether to sort on ascending or descending order. The following SORT statement is for the IBM sort:

SORT FIELDS=(1,4,CH,A,20,10,CH,D)

The (1,4,CH,A) tells the system that the first sort key begins in byte 1, is 4 bytes long, is in CHaracter form, and is to be in Ascending order. The (20,10,CH,D) specifies that the second sort key begins in byte 20, is 10 bytes long, is in CHaracter form, and is to be in Descending order. Such a SORT statement and a few JCL statements are all that are necessary to sort a file.

COBOL SORT Verb

The COBOL sort requires more coding than the sort utility, but it is still relatively simple. You describe a sort file, along with a sort record that names the record files. Then you code the SORT verb in the PROCEDURE DIVISION of the program. The SORT verb names the fields upon which to sort, in the proper order.

The following example illustrates the COBOL SORT verb. TRANS-FILE is sorted on ascending order on TRANS-NAME and TRANS-AGE, and on descending order on TRANS-HEIGHT. The sorted records are written into NEW-TRANS-FILE. (SORT-TRANS is the sort file name and must be described in the FILE SECTION.)

```
SORT SORT-TRANS
    ON ASCENDING KEY TRANS-NAME, TRANS-AGE
    ON DESCENDING KEY TRANS-HEIGHT
    USING TRANS-FILE
    GIVING NEW-TRANS-FILE.
```

The COBOL sort allows you to name a sort input procedure to supply the records to the sort, and to name a sort output procedure to receive the sorted records from the sort. The sort procedures enables you to sort a table contained within a program and store it back in sorted order, something not possible with an external sort. The sort input procedure also allows you to select out records before they are sorted, which speeds up the sort.

Coding a Sort

The third and least desirable method of sorting is to write your own sort in COBOL or whatever language you use. If you do, know that it will probably be less efficient than the manufacturer-provided sort, be more likely to contain errors, and be much more difficult to write. Perhaps the only reason for writing your own sort is if there is no other means of doing the sort.

The following example in COBOL illustrates a bubble sort, the simplest sorting technique. In the bubble sort, the first table element is compared to each successive element. For an ascending sort, the two elements are switched if the first element is greater than the second. This "bubbles" the largest value to the end of the table. The procedure is repeated for the second through the next to last element so that the entire table ends up in the desired order. The following example illustrates a bubble sort in which the 1000 elements of the table AMOUNT are sorted into ascending order.

```
77  SWAP                 PIC S9(7)V99 COMP-3.
```
[SWAP is a data item used to swap table elements]
```
01  A-TABLE.
    05  X-AMT            PIC S9(4) COMP.
    05  Y-AMT            PIC S9(4) COMP.
    05  AMOUNT           PIC S9(7)V99 COMP-3
                         OCCURS 1000 TIMES.
```
[AMOUNT is the table to sort; two subscripts are needed for the sort]
```
B10-BUBBLE-SORT.
****  BUBBLE SORT TO PLACE TABLE AMOUNT INTO
                                      ASCENDING ORDER.
      PERFORM B10-PART-A
      VARYING X-AMT FROM 1 BY 1
      UNTIL X-AMT > 999.
****  EXIT
B10-PART-A.
      PERFORM B10-PART-B
      VARYING Y-AMT FROM X-AMT BY 1
      UNTIL Y-AMT > 1000.
****  EXIT
B10-PART-B.
      IF AMOUNT (X-AMT) > AMOUNT (Y-AMT)
          THEN MOVE AMOUNT (Y-AMT) TO SWAP
               MOVE AMOUNT (X-AMT) TO AMOUNT (Y-AMT)
               MOVE SWAP TO AMOUNT (X-AMT).
****  EXIT
****  END OF B10-BUBBLE-SORT
```

MERGE

A merge combines several files sorted in the same order into a single file in the same sort order. Merging yields the same results as if the several files were concatenated as input to a normal sort, but merging is more efficient because the input files are known to be already in the proper sort order.

Like the sort, a merge can be done using the system sort utility with its MERGE statement, by using the COBOL MERGE verb, or by coding your own merge. Again you should try to use the system sort utility first, then the COBOL MERGE, and code our own merge as a last resort. Figure 17 illustrates a merge.

The pseudocode for programming your own merge is as follows:

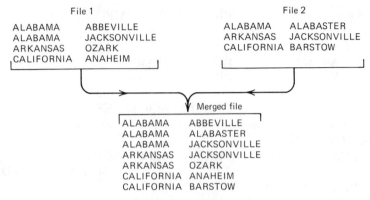

Figure 17 Merge.

Read file-1 into record-1
    at end move high-values to record-1.
Read file-2 into record-2
    at end move high-values to record-2.

.
.
.

Read file-n into record-n
    at end move high-values to record-n.
Do until eof all files.
    If key-1 < = key-1 and key-2 and . . . and key-n
      then write merged-file from record-1
        read file-1 into record-1
          at end move high-values to record-1
    Else if key-2 < = key-1 and key-3 and . . . and key-n
      then write merged-file from record-2
        read file-2 into record-2
          at end move high-values to record-2

.
.
.

    Else if key-n < = key-1 and key-2 and . . . and key-n-1
      then write merged file from record-n
        read file-n into record-n
          at end move high-values to record-n.
    End.

SORT EFFICIENCY

Sorts are relatively expensive and can account for a large portion of the running cost of a system. In searching for ways to reduce a system's running cost, look carefully at the sorts. Sorts are heavily I/O bound. Block the sort input and output as high as possible. The manufacturer may provide ways to optimize a sort's performance. Assuming that a job's cost is a function of CPU time and I/O count, the cost of a sort increases exponentially with the number of records sorted; it costs more than twice as much to sort 1000 records than it costs to sort 500 records. The cost of a sort also increases proportionally to the record length and the number of sort keys. It costs more to sort a 1000 byte record than a 400 byte record.

The number of records and the record length can often be reduced for a sort. Suppose that a file containing 10,000 fixed-length records of 1000 bytes must be sorted to produce a report, but that only 5000 records are selected for the report with 100 bytes of each record being used. Such a file would be relatively expensive to sort, requiring the reading, sorting, and writing out of 10,000 records, and reading the 10,000 records back into the report program. Each record contains 1000 bytes, resulting in a total of 30 million bytes transmitted and 10,000 records of 1000 bytes sorted. To reduce this, we could read in the 10,000 records in a sort input procedure, select only the 5000 records needed, move the 100 bytes needed for the report to the sort record, sort the 5000 records with an internal sort, and write the report in a sort output procedure. The result is 10 million bytes read and 5000 records of 100 bytes sorted. The two methods are summarized in the following table:

Full Sort	Selecting Records
• Read 10,000 records of 1000 bytes	• Read 10,000 records of 1000 bytes
• Sort 10,000 records of 1000 bytes	• Sort 5000 records of 100 bytes
• Write 10,000 records of 1000 bytes	• Produce report in sort output procedure.
• Read 10,000 records of 1000 bytes in report program	*Total:* 10 million bytes transmitted, sort 5000 records of 100 bytes
Total: 30 million bytes transmitted, sort 10,000 records of 1000 bytes	

ELEVEN

Reports

Without doubt the report is the most volatile part of a program. Since much of the change in computer programs results from the catalytic effect of data upon the user and it is the report that displays the data to the user, it is no surprise that reports are often changed. We will be looking at ways to make them easier to change, but first let us examine a typical report and how it might have evolved.

ANATOMY OF A REPORT

In order to understand the problems encountered in reports, let us examine a report from the viewpoint of a user. Perhaps this will make it clearer why reports get changed so much. For this we need an example with which we can personally identify. Let us suppose that we have a file containing a record of each financial transaction in our personal lives, including expenses and income. We would probably want to classify the expenses into such categories as rent, food, vices, and clothing. Then we can run a report each month and see how we did financially. Our first cut at this might be to produce a simple listing in COBOL such as the following:

JOB	AJAX APPAREL	PAYCHECK	0008623
TAX	FEDERAL	INCOME	174623P
RENT	BOB'S BATH HOUSE	SHOWER	000005&

There are several things typical about this report so far. It is generated from a file, with the information in each line in the report coming from an individual record. The data in the record is hierarchical, with the levels of hierarchy being the category, the vendor, and the item.

The 0008623 is actually $86.23, the 174623P is actually −17,462.37 (unless told otherwise, COBOL combines the sign with the right-most digit to produce a new character), and the 00005& is actually −.50. Obviously we need to edit the numbers to suppress leading zeros, print the decimal point, print the minus sign, and it would be nice to insert the commas. The listing now looks as follows:

JOB	AJAX APPAREL	PAYCHECK	86.23
TAX	FEDERAL	INCOME	−17,462.37
RENT	BOB'S BATH HOUSE	SHOWER	−0.50

The lines in a report containing the lowest level of data are termed detail lines to distinguish them from the summary lines we shall soon encounter. Now let us see what changes we might want to make. A glance at the listing tells us that it would look nicer with a page heading. And if we are doing a page heading, we should include a page number, column headings, and a date so that we can know the month. Of course, we would want the page heading to be repeated at the top of each new page. This necessitates counting the lines on the page as they are printed so that we can tell when a new page is needed.

Almost every report you write will need both a page and a line counter. The page counter is initialized to zero and incremented just prior to printing the page heading. The line counter is initialized to zero and incremented just prior to printing each line. It is also reset to zero with each new page.

With the page heading, our report might look as follows:

		MONTHLY FINANCE REPORT	PAGE 1
		MONTH OF JUNE	
CATEGORY	VENDOR	ITEM	AMOUNT
VICE	HARRY'S LIQUOR	CHEAP SCOTCH	−2.25
VICE	HARRY'S LIQUOR	OVERCHARGE REFUND	0.45

Notice that the page heading contains variable information: the page number and the month. This is typical, and the variable information might come from run parameters, from system-provided information such as the run date, and from the next record to be printed. Thus a page heading may also act as a control heading. For example, we might want to start a new page with each new CATEGORY.

The previous detail lines show up a problem. We have not really distinguished expenses from revenue. We have been using the sign to distinguish between them, but it does not always work. We can solve the problem by adding the information to each detail line as follows:

CATEGORY	VENDOR	ITEM		AMOUNT
JOB	AJAX APPAREL	COP PETTY CASH	REVENUE	12.33
JOB	AJAX APPAREL	RETURN PETTY CASH	REVENUE	−12.13

Better yet, the categories of expense and revenue can be made column headings.

CATEGORY	VENDOR		REVENUE	EXPENSE
FOOD	MABEL'S MUSHROOMS	LUNCH		6.26
MEDICAL	MERCY GENERAL	PUMP STOMACH		66.23

We might next decide that some summarization is in order. We would probably want to summarize by category and vendor. And we would certainly want a grand total. In order to print the summarization lines, we need to keep running totals for each column (revenue and expense) and for each of the levels being summarized (grand total, category, and vendor). The input file must now be sorted on category and vendor to produce the report. The report might now look like the following:

CATEGORY	VENDOR	ITEM	REVENUE	EXPENSE
FOOD	PIERRE'S	DINNER		132.65
FOOD	PIERRE'S	WASH DISHES	132.65	
FOOD	PIERRE'S	DINNER		3.75
FOOD	PIERRE'S	TOTAL	132.65	136.40
	.			
	.			
	.			
FOOD	TOTAL		189.65	10,456.23
	.			
	.			
GRAND TOTAL			544.32	22,721.48

The summary lines are termed control footings because they occur after a control break, that is, after the value of a key in the hierarchy changes. The control footing break occurs after a detail line is printed. When a control footing break occurs, control breaks must be forced on all lower control items in the hierarchy. The order in which the control footing breaks occur is from minor to major. That is, if FOOD is the category in the previous record and RENT the category in the current record, we have a control break for the CATEGORY, but first we must force a control break for VENDOR (minor) and then do the control break for CATEGORY (major). An end-of-file or end-of-report is treated like a control footing break and must force a control break from minor (VENDOR) to major (CATEGORY) of all the hierarchy levels being reported, before the grand total is printed.

Since we can have both revenues and expenses in the same summarization line, we would probably like to see their total in the report. Totaling numbers in the same line is termed cross footing. The report now looks as follows:

CATEGORY	VENDOR	ITEM	REVENUE	EXPENSE	NET
VICE	HIALEAH	5TH RACE		2.00	
VICE	HIALEAH	5TH RACE	1,000.00		
VICE	HIALEAH	TOTAL	1,000.00	2.00	998.00

The next thing we might do is eliminate some of the redundant data. The category and vendor names need only be printed the first time they appear, and instead of printing them on the detail lines, we can print them by themselves in indented form. Printing the names necessitates a control break, and since the information is printed before the detail lines, it is termed a control heading. The report now looks as follows:

CATEGORY	VENDOR	ITEM	REVENUE	EXPENSE	NET
TRANSPORTATION	KHOMEINI OIL	GASOLINE		226.25	
		FAN BELT		6.79	
		GASOLINE		106.36	
		TOTAL		339.40	
	CITY	BUS		0.80	
		SUBWAY		0.97	
		TOTAL		1.77	
TOTAL TRANSPORTATION				341.17	

The report looks clearer because it is less cluttered. Printing each heading on a separate line permits indenting each level in the hierarchy only a few spaces to free space across the page. Indenting also shows the hierarchical relationship of the data. The report could have been indented as follows if we needed more space for columns:

TRANSPORTATION
    KHOMEINI OIL
        GASOLINE

The control heading is printed when a control item in the next record to be printed changes value from the previous record. It is printed before the detail line, but takes its values from the detail record. A control heading break for an item in a hierarchy requires that control breaks also be forced for all lower level control items in the hierarchy, in the order from major to minor. Thus in the previous example a change in the CATEGORY (major) caused TRANSPORTATION to be printed, and then a control break is forced for the VENDOR (minor) causing KHOMEINI OIL to be printed. The first detail line printed at the start of a report must cause a control heading break for all levels of the hierarchy.

Now let us step back and generalize the items that went into the report. There are many different types of reports, but most business application reports will have the form shown in Figure 18.

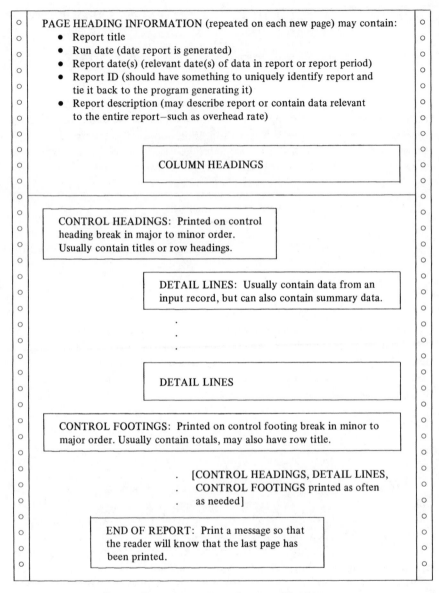

PAGE HEADING INFORMATION (repeated on each new page) may contain:
- Report title
- Run date (date report is generated)
- Report date(s) (relevant date(s) of data in report or report period)
- Report ID (should have something to uniquely identify report and tie it back to the program generating it)
- Report description (may describe report or contain data relevant to the entire report—such as overhead rate)

COLUMN HEADINGS

CONTROL HEADINGS: Printed on control heading break in major to minor order. Usually contain titles or row headings.

DETAIL LINES: Usually contain data from an input record, but can also contain summary data.

DETAIL LINES

CONTROL FOOTINGS: Printed on control footing break in minor to major order. Usually contain totals, may also have row title.

. [CONTROL HEADINGS, DETAIL LINES,
. CONTROL FOOTINGS printed as often
. as needed]

END OF REPORT: Print a message so that the reader will know that the last page has been printed.

Figure 18 Components of a generalized report.

134

REPORT PROBLEMS

There are several variations to the basic report format which often crop up.
These and several common problems are explained in the following sections.

Printing Two Up

Sometimes when there are few columns, you may wish to print several logical lines on one physical line. Suppose that we are printing addresses "two
up" on prepasted label forms. The easiest way to do this is to print left to
right, top to bottom, as shown in Figure 19.

This presents no particular problem other than formatting each line
from two input records. However, if the columns must be in sort order, it
becomes more difficult. The last line on the page is continued at the top of
the same page, indented to the right, as shown in Figure 20.

The easiest way to accomplish this is to establish a table containing all
the data to appear on a page. The table is filled by reading the input records
and storing the data to be printed consecutively into the table. If an end-of-
file occurs within the page, the remaining entries in the table can be blanked

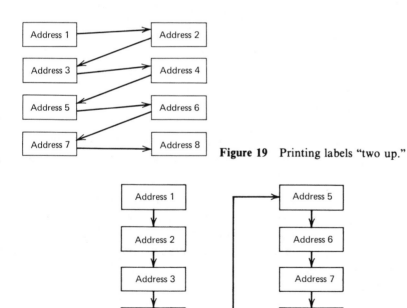

Figure 19 Printing labels "two up."

Figure 20 Printing labels in sort order.

out. Each line is then formatted by moving data to it from the table. If we were printing a line in the previous example, we would move table (*n*) and table (*n* + 4) to the print line. This technique can be extended to print any number of logical lines on a single physical line.

Eliminating Unnecessary Information

Next to forest fires and the Japanese beetle, the greatest menace to our trees is to be pulped into paper for computer printout. Paper will become increasingly expensive. You should design reports so that paper will not be wasted. Eliminate unnecessary information in a report to both save paper and make the report more comprehensible. For example, a line containing all zeros might not be printed, and a total line might be eliminated if only one item goes into the totals.

```
                    HOURS
ENG DEPT
    JOHN DOE         0
    MARY ROE        10
    DEPT TOTAL      10
```

Can be better presented as:

```
                    HOURS
ENG DEPT
    MARY ROE        10
```

The page heading need not be repeated on each page if it remains unchanged. Print it on the first page, and use an abbreviated page heading thereafter.

Exception reporting is the best way to reduce the volume of reports. Most reports contain information that is of little interest and seldom used. Often you can get by with printing only the exceptional data on a regular basis, relegating the full report to request. If you were an administrative assistant preparing a weekly roster of employees, you might list only those who are leaving or have just been hired.

Another way to save paper is to use microfilm or microfiche. This not only saves paper, but it also saves storage space. The disadvantage is that it is more difficult to read. You need a viewer to read the material, and you have to mount it in the viewer and find the page you want. You can not take it home at night and mark it all up with pencil as with printed output. But for archival data, microfilm and microfiche are excellent.

Page Footing

Sometimes you must print lines at the bottom of a page after the last report line on the page has been printed. These lines are termed "page footings." For example, we might want to print "CONTINUED ON THE NEXT PAGE" after the last report line on the page. This is done by using the line counter to space down to the bottom of the page. If we want to print the page footing on line 60 and the line counter points to line 52 after the last line on the page has been printed, we must print eight blank lines (lines 52 through 59) to space down before printing the page footing.

Report Heading

The report heading consists of information printed before the main body of a report. It can be printed on a separate page before the report itself, or it can be printed as the first page heading, with the remaining page headings being abbreviated to save paper. The report heading can contain such information as handling and distribution instructions. It might also contain the selection criteria, the sort order, and other assumptions that went into the report.

Report Footing

The report footing consists of information printed after the main body of the report. It can be continued on the same page as the report body, or it can be printed on a separate page. It might contain information such as hash and control totals. A report footing is also a convenient place to print run statistics such as the number of records read and written for each file. It can further provide warning messages, such as noting when a table is close to overflowing, or, by computing from the number of records written, it can tell when a tape reel came close to being filled.

All reports should have something to indicate the end of the report, such as an "END OF REPORT" message, so that you can tell at a glance that you have all of the pages. (The consecutive page numbers tell if a page is missing, but they can not tell which page is the last.)

Fitting on the Page

Perhaps the most common problem in printing reports is exceeding the columns on a page. What can you do if you need 150 columns and the print page is limited to 132? There are several alternatives:

- Squeeze any blanks from between columns. Columns should not be run together, but often several blanks can be squeezed down to one:

23   15   64.7

squeezed down to:

23   15   64.7

- Eliminate the nonessential. In a print line 132 characters is a considerable amount of information, and there is likely to be something printed
that is nonessential. For example, if three columns contain a starting
date, an ending date, and a duration, all of the information is contained
in any two of the columns. The third column may be convenient, but it
is also redundant.
- Print two or more lines, staggering the columns:

	START DATE	END DATE	FIRST 6-MO	SECOND 6-MO
DEPARTMENT 115				
JOHN DOE	01/01/82	12/31/83	100,000.00	250,000.00

by staggering columns we get:

	START DATE	FIRST 6-MO
	END DATE	SECOND 6-MO
DEPARTMENT 115		
JOHN DOE	01/01/82	100,000.00
	12/31/83	250,000.00

- Print two reports, where the second report is a logical continuation of
the columns of the first, so that the two reports placed side by side form
a complete report. Print all the page and column headings of the second report too, so that it can stand by itself. In practice, people will not
lay the reports side by side because it is awkward. The second report can
be printed on the following page by storing it in a table and printing it
from the table after having printed the first page, or it can be printed as
a separate file so that it forms a completely separate report.
- Print each row heading on a separate line, indenting to show the hierarchy, rather than printing them on the same line:

CALIFORNIA   MARIN   MILL CITY   200.45   345,628

can be indented to:

CALIFORNIA
    MARIN
        MILL CITY   200.45   345,628

Printing Totals Before Detail

It is logical to print totals at the end of a column of numbers, and this is easier to program, but managers may want the totals at the top of the page because to them the total is the most important item, and they want to see it first. (This type of manager is usually referred to as a "bottom line" person.)

If a report must print totals at the top of the page before the detail lines, there are three solutions. First, you can store the lines of data in a table, total the table, and then print the lines from the table. However, this does not work when the report becomes large because of the size of the table that would be required. The second solution is to pass through the file twice, the first time to compute the totals and the second time to print the report. However, this is slow and gets complicated if there are many subtotals to compute.

The third alternative is to write the lines into a file with a sort key appended containing the report, page, and line number. When the last line is written and the total line is formed, it is given a page and line number to cause it to be sorted in front of the detail lines. After the report is completed, the lines can be sorted, the file read, the sort key dropped, and the actual report printed.

Underlining

Sometimes a column of numbers must be underlined to denote a total, and the total double underlined to highlight it:

        1432
        <u>3216</u>
        <u>5648</u>

A single underline is accomplished by printing the underscore character (_) and suppressing line spacing. This overprints the underscore on the previous line, underlining the item: <u>3216</u>. The double underline is accomplished by printing a line of equal signs (=) on the next line: <u>5648</u>

Underlining numbers is one of those nice touches of marginal value that make programming difficult. Avoid it if you can.

WRITING REPORTS

Most of the data in reports is hierarchical, and the rows and columns are summarized to various hierarchical levels. This can present some sticky logical problems, and report programs often become complicated. Then they are difficult to change. Normal computer language statements have only the primitive facility for printing a single line. They know nothing about column positions, page headings, control breaks, control totals, and line positions. However, a good report writer does. A report writer is an invaluable tool that can speed up programming and make reports easier to maintain and change.

The COBOL language report writer is, on the whole, excellent. But for reasons not entirely clear, it is little used. Partly this may be because programmers worry about efficiency and believe that they can code a report more efficiently than the COBOL report writer. They probably can, just as they can also write reports to be even more efficient in assembly language. But this argument is specious. Programmer productivity has stayed relatively constant for the past two decades while computer hardware has twice gone through order of magnitude increases in performance. The CPU of 20 years ago that occupied an entire room and dimmed the lights in the neighborhood when it was turned on is now cheap enough and small enough to put in children's toys.

Another reason that people do not use the report writer is that they must learn to use it, and since few others may be using it, it can get lonesome, tracking down problems and trying to find answers to questions. Nonetheless, you should learn to use it as it will make you more productive.

Most of the coding for the COBOL report writer is done in the DATA DIVISION in the form of layouts and specifications. Not only does this eliminate much of the tricky programming, it also documents the report and makes it easier to change. Extensive report changes that would take days of programming and debugging to accomplish in the PROCEDURE DIVISION can be made by simple changes to specifications in the DATA DIVISION.

A comprehensive description of the COBOL report writer is contained in the author's book, *Advanced ANS COBOL with Structured Programming*, published by John Wiley & Sons, Inc.

DESIGNING REPORTS

Reports are not designed in a vacuum. They have a symbiotic relationship to the data in a system. Reports are limited by the data available in the files, and, in turn, the data in the files is often dictated by the requirements of a report.

Since the needs of reports may dictate the data in a new system, the design of a report should come early in the design of the system. In fact, the reporting needs generally dictate the need for a system, and your job is often to work back to determine the data needed, which in turn sets the input requirements. You should provide the customers with sample reports or layouts as soon as possible so that they can make changes early in the design.

The design of a report usually begins with a rough description of the data to be reported. Given this general idea of what the report is to contain, you must fill in the details, including the page headings, rows and columns, column sizes, and so on. The usual tool for laying out a report is a report layout sheet, a form marked off with 132 characters per line and 66 lines per page. When the report layout sheet is completed, it is then used as documentation.

However, in practice the report layout sheet is a poor design tool because it is so difficult to change. As soon as you show the report layout sheet to the user, it will get changed. On the report layout sheet you pencil in the exact columns where the data are to appear, and if you have 10 columns in a report and want to shift the first column over one position, all the columns must be shifted over, and you essentially have to redo the entire layout sheet. A couple of iterations of this, and you will be happy never to see a report layout sheet again.

A better way to lay out reports is to simply type them on a regular sheet of paper turned on its side. An elite typewriter gives a page size of 51 by 130 characters and a pica typewriter a size of 48 by 105. Figure 21 is such an example. Now the layout sheet is easy to duplicate and distribute in memos, and it is also easy to change, using the cut and paste technique. The typed report does not show the exact column positions, but these are not needed. In the design stage the customer should be made to focus on the information contained in the report and on the general format.

You should get a layout of the report into the customer's hands as soon as possible. Everything is abstract until the customers see the report. It is at this point, where the customers have something concrete to focus on, that they begin to understand exactly what they want. With the report as a catalyst, the customers may make changes—many changes. The design of a report is an iterative process, and it is here that a simple typed report layout that can be cut and spliced can save days of effort.

The report layout sheet may come in handy in actually formatting the report for programming, if there is a need to position each line and column. However, it may be as easy to compute the column positions from the typed layout form and pencil them in for programming.

Although the report layout sheet is often used for documentation, it is again poor because it is difficult to change. With a report writer, the programming changes are often easier than redoing the report layout sheet to keep the documentation up to date. The simplest way to document a report

REPORT ID: XXXXXXX

DIVISION SALES REPORT
BY DEPARTMENT BY PROJECT
PERIOD: XX/XX/XX TO XX/XX/XX

PAGE XXX

DEPARTMENT/PROJECT	CURRENT MONTH SALES	LAST MONTH SALES	YEAR-TO-DATE SALES	LAST Y-T-D SALES
XXXXXXXXX				
XXXXXXXXXX	XXX,XXX.XX	XXX,XXX.XX	XXX,XXX.XX	XXX,XXX.XX
.	.	.	.	.
.	.	.	.	.
.	.	.	.	.
TOTAL	XXX,XXX.XX	XXX,XXX.XX	XXX,XXX.XX	XXX,XXX.XX
XXXXXXXXX				
XXXXXXXXXX	XXX,XXX.XX	XXX,XXX.XX	XXX,XXX.XX	XXX,XXX.XX
.	.	.	.	.
.	.	.	.	.
.	.	.	.	.
TOTAL	XXX,XXX.XX	XXX,XXX.XX	XXX,XXX.XX	XXX,XXX.XX
GRAND TOTAL	XXX,XXX.XX	XXX,XXX.XX	XXX,XXX.XX	XXX,XXX.XX

Figure 21 Typical report layout.

is to file a sample copy of it. Each time the report is changed, you file a new sample copy from the test run. The entire report need not be filed, but only representative pages to show the format. The specific line and column positions in the sample report can be determined either with a business forms ruler marked off in column positions or by laying a translucent report layout sheet over the report.

PRINTER CONSIDERATIONS

Line printers print a line at a time on continuous form paper, which stacks roughly 2700 pages per foot. The paper is normally 14 by 11 inches, with 66 lines per page (six lines per inch) and 132 characters per line (10 characters per inch). Some printers allow eight lines per inch for 88 lines per page. Line widths of 100, 120, 136, 160, 163, and 204 characters are also found. Paper also comes in an $8\frac{1}{2}$ by 11 inch size with 66 or 88 lines per page, depending on the number of lines per inch, and 85 characters per line. Other paper sizes are also available, but these are the most common.

Although the normal 14 by 11 inch paper can contain 66 lines per page, most installations set the printer carriage control to print fewer lines, usually 60. The result is a few blank lines at the top and bottom of the page. This is done not only for aesthetics, but also so that the operators do not have to be so careful in aligning the print line to the paper's perforation.

Slow impact printers print at rates from 100 to 600 lines per minute, and fast impact printers print at rates from 1100 to 3000 lines per minute. Very fast nonimpact printers are capable of rates of up to 13,360 lines per minute.

Microfilm is sometimes used as an alternative to the printer. The output is "printed" on microfilm rather than paper, and besides being faster, it condenses large stacks of paper down into small amounts of microfilm with no special programming. Several pages of microfilm are often placed on a single microfiche for convenient storage. The drawback of computer output microfilm (COM) is that it takes a special device to print the microfilm and a special viewer to read it.

Multiple report copies can be made either by printing the report several times or by using multiple part paper. Printing a report several times makes each copy as legible as the first and does not require special paper. However, for long reports in which several copies are required, this can tie up a printer for a long time. Alternatively you can print on multiple part paper to make several copies at one time. Multiple part paper comes with interleaved carbons, and up to eight copies can be made, with the last copy retaining some legibility. Multiple part paper has several drawbacks. The paper costs more than the same number of copies of regular paper, each successive copy is less legible, the ink in the copies smears and comes off on your hands, the forms must be mounted and dismounted from the printer, and the carbons must be removed from the paper. A deleaving machine is available to remove the carbons as it is a messy job to do by hand. Even with the deleaving machine, the paper may jam and tear a few pages.

One further way of making copies is with a continuous form copying machine. This is like an office copier, but it accepts the continuous form computer paper after it comes off the printer. (Some copiers can accept tape input.) The 14 by 11 inch paper is reduced to a more convenient 8½ by 11 inch size, and several copies may be made.

Special forms can also be made up into many sizes, and are most widely used to print checks. The special forms can have anything preprinted on them, and may come in colors and multiple part paper. Never use special forms unless you must because they are more expensive and the forms must be mounted, aligned, and dismounted on the printer. They also make reports inflexible because a report change may require designing a new form, with the lead time to have it made up and delivered.

TWELVE

On-Line

Computing is moving more and more to on-line operation in which you address a computer directly through a terminal. The reason is simple— productivity. On-line systems give faster response than traditional batch-oriented systems. An on-site terminal can save a walk down to the computer room. A remote terminal connected to the main computer by communications lines can do in seconds what would take days to do by mail. On-line systems are more powerful and more enjoyable than batch systems. Aside from the complexity of providing the on-line systems, their main drawback is cost. But with increasing personnel costs and decreasing hardware costs they become more affordable each year.

USING ON-LINE SERVICES

You will encounter on-line systems in two ways—as a user of on-line services and as a programmer providing on-line services to users. Your use of on-line services will include remote job entry, the use of a text editor, and perhaps the use of a debugging compiler. These uses will be in support of your normal programming language. As a provider of on-line services, you may program in COBOL, which has a communications facility, but more likely you will use an on-line language such as BASIC, APL, or a specialized language provided by the computer manufacturer. You may work on the main computer, on a minicomputer that communicates with the main computer, or even on a minicomputer that is a part of a remote terminal.

The Text Editor

A text editor is a facility that allows you to examine lines of text, edit or change individual lines, add and delete lines, and move lines or groups of lines. In short, it does word processing. The text can be any written material, such as a source program, a manual, a report, or a memo. In addition to simple changes, many text editors provide even more powerful editing features, such as changing all instances of a word to something else. Thus if you are cleaning up a COBOL source program and you want to change an identifier name from TAX to STATE-TAX, you simply instruct the text editor to do so.

Making changes to text may be slightly more difficult with a text editor than with pencil, paper, scissors, and tape. The advantage of a text editor is that a clean, new listing can be produced with no effort. If you change a word in a memo, you do not have to retype the whole thing; you simply make a new listing. You can either list it on your terminal, if your terminal has hard copy capability, or you can print it on the computer's high-speed printer. For full word processing, the high-speed printer needs both uppercase and lowercase characters.

Text editors can also be used for information retrieval. Many text editors can operate on standard sequential files. Thus you can list an entire data file, list only specified lines in the file, or list all lines containing specified items of information, such as all lines in a source program containing the word STATE-TAX. Furthermore, a text editor that operates on standard files can be used as an alternative to a file dump. Rather than printing an entire file, you retrieve and examine it with the text editor.

The text editor does more than just update text; it organizes it. It can maintain source programs, the COPY library, subroutines, JCL, utility programs, and even test data. Your naming convention can indicate the system to which the materials belong. A properly chosen name can also indicate the version number of the materials. You will often need to maintain the current production version of a source program, the previous production version, and a new version being tested. Consequently a text editor becomes almost a librarian for production systems. Even documentation can be maintained on-line with the text editor.

Remote Job Entry

Remote job entry allows jobs to be submitted from a terminal, and also to receive your output at a terminal. It can be a card reader and printer located away from the computer, but more usually your job is stored as card images in a file on the computer's direct-access storage, and you use a terminal to submit the file to the computer. The output is then saved by the operating system as a file rather than being printed, and you can retrieve it, examine it, and then either discard it or instruct the system to print it. Obviously remote job entry can save an enormous amount of paper.

Remote job entry takes much of the inertia out of submitting batch jobs, and can significantly reduce turnaround time. In a typical batch job you first stop by the keypunch room to keypunch your changes. Then you insert them in your card deck. After this you walk over to the computer room and submit your card deck. Now you walk back to your office and wait. Later, when you think your job may be done, you again walk down to the computer room to retrieve your output. Now you find that your job never got into execution because of a JCL error, and you start the entire cycle over.

With remote job entry, you change your source program from a terminal and submit it. Then you use the remote job entry facilities to monitor your job's progress through the system, to see how many jobs are ahead of it in the queue, and when your job is completed. After the job has run, you retrieve the output from your terminal and scan the lines of error messages to discover the JCL error. You then scratch the output rather than print it, retrieve your program again, change the JCL, and resubmit it—all of this without leaving your office.

One danger with remote job entry systems is cost. It is not that they are inherently expensive, but they can be like walking into a casino that accepts credit cards. Expenses mount rapidly. The fast response of on-line systems can also lead to bad work habits. The longer the turnaround time, the more incentive there is not to waste a run. Consequently on-line systems take some self-discipline.

All in all, a good text editor, coupled with the remote job entry facility, is perhaps the most important programming development of the past decade. If your installation does not have both, consider changing jobs.

Incremental Compilers

Another tool you may occasionally use is an incremental compiler. An incremental compiler interprets each language statement just prior to executing it, rather than compiling all statements at the same time. This allows you to execute your program a statement at a time, examine variables as the program executes, stop the execution at any time, change statements, and resume execution. Incremental compilers permit programming in the conversational mode.

There are two general types of incremental compilers. The first are programming languages such as BASIC, APL, and derivations of PL/I designed especially for on-line use. They have statements to demand input from the keyboard and to print output on the terminal. They are excellent for most programming problems except the handling of large amounts of data. However, most business applications involve handling large amounts of data, so do not throw away your COBOL manual.

Because incremental compilers do not compile, but are interpreted as they execute, they execute less efficiently than batch compilers. However, more and more computers are supporting these languages in the hardware rather than by software, and they are becoming more efficient. They can be more efficient than a batch compiler for simple problems because of their quick turnaround and debugging aids. They would be terribly inefficient to process a million records in a tape file, but this is a batch application, not an on-line application.

The second type of incremental compiler is the debugging compiler, which supports a traditional language such as COBOL, FORTRAN, or PL/I. Its purpose is to facilitate the debugging of a computer program by allowing the program to be stopped, variables examined, changes made, as well as permitting the other facilities made possible by an incremental compiler. Debugging compilers can be very useful, but they can also be overkill. The ability to execute your program a statement at a time and examine selected variables is great when you are tracking down a tough logic problem, but a problem that merits this approach is rare. Usually you want to see how your program processes a few hundred records, and for this you do not want to examine each statement as it executes.

A further drawback to debugging compilers is that when you have completed your debugging, you must compile the program under the batch compiler, which may result in conversion problems. In theory there should be none, but you must make tests to ensure that this is so.

PROVIDING ON-LINE SERVICES

Those who depend on the computer for information often become heavy users of on-line systems. Rather than filling out input forms and submitting them to data entry, they can enter the information directly to the computer from a terminal. Rather than receiving stacks of printed output that will never be read, they can select what they want and list it on their terminal.

Despite the advantages of user on-line systems, there are several disadvantages. Everyone has skill with a pencil; not everyone has typing skill. Corrections made with pencil and eraser are easier than corrections made with a terminal—you must tell a terminal what to do. With pencil and eraser you make the correction directly. An input form is more portable. People can fill out input forms at their desk, whereas they may have to move their work to a terminal room for on-line input. Then they may have to await an available terminal. Hardware and software problems do not trouble pencil and paper as they do an on-line terminal.

It takes more programming effort to support on-line input and output than it does for pencil and paper. Because the development of on-line systems is generally more fun than that of batch systems, inappropriate applications often occur. If there is no need for the fast response or the power that operating in a conversational mode brings, do not go on-line. And do not go on-line if the hardware and software response and availability are not dependable.

CHARACTERISTICS OF ON-LINE SYSTEMS

On-line systems are not just fast batch. They operate under different considerations. The type of terminal, the response time, the impact on system availability, and the remoteness of the user, all make a difference. On-line also permits conversational systems. The immediate response to inquiries that on-line systems provide allows people to think and act differently than they do with batch systems. An on-line system can prompt for missing information, respond to questions, and make suggestions. With a batch system, all the input decisions must be made before the run is submitted. Decisions can be made during the running of an on-line system and be based on intermediate output.

Terminals

There are three types of on-line terminals: typewriter, cathode ray tube (CRT), and graphical. The typewriter is one dimensional. It types a single character at a time to form a single line at a time. The user must respond to each line as it is typed.

The CRT can also be used like a typewriter to type a single line at a time and await a response. But it is really two dimensional. You can display several lines, filling up a screen, before the user needs to respond. Since the user may respond to any of several lines, a cursor, generally an underscore (_) character, is provided to indicate where the next character typed will be placed. You can move the cursor around on the screen with special control keys, in addition to the tab, space, backspace, and carriage return.

CRTs are faster than typewriter devices. Some CRTs are very fast, filling an entire screen almost immediately. A CRT with this speed adds yet another dimension to the device. Rather than dealing with lines, you begin to deal with pages. There is a tremendous difference between listing information a line at a time as you do on a typewriter, and listing a page at a time on the screen. In effect, you are looking through a larger window. Since things are always more understandable in context, the larger view of the screen enhances your understanding by providing more lines of context. Looking at one line of a program does not tell you much. Looking at an entire page makes more sense.

The advantages of typewriter terminals are that they provide hard copy, are generally cheaper, and may also function as regular typewriters. Their disadvantages are their relatively slow speed and their noise. The advantage of CRTs is their speed and ability to work with a page of information. Their disadvantages are their cost and the amount of programming required to support them. Some CRT terminals have hardware to provide hardcopy, but usually hardcopy is obtained by routing the CRT display to the host computer's printer.

Graphical terminals are like CRTs in that they can display a full screen of several lines, but in addition they can draw lines and plot points. Unlike the CRT in which you display one line after another until you fill up the screen, each character, each point, each end point of a line, and each line of text can be positioned by an x, y coordinate. The characters and lines can be moved about on the screen under program control by changing their x, y coordinates. This permits dynamic displays in which the images are moved under program control.

Input can come from a keyboard, but it may also come from a light pen with which you touch the screen directly. The graphical input can be characters of text entered by the keyboard, or an x, y position obtained from a light pen. Despite their power, graphical terminals have a limited, specialized use. They are not general purpose programming tools in the way that typewriter and CRT terminals are.

Terminals come in both "smart" and "dumb" varieties. The terms are not meant to be pejorative, but to indicate that a smart terminal has some processing capability whereas a dumb terminal does not. With a dumb terminal, whatever you type goes directly to the computer. Output from the computer is typed directly on the terminal.

A smart terminal usually contains a buffer, may have file storage capability, and may also be programmed. A smart terminal can take a large load off the host computer and greatly reduce the amount of information transmitted between the terminal and the host computer. As an example, the host computer might send an entire file to the terminal. The terminal processor could then be used to view portions of the output. Likewise on input, the terminal processor might have editing capability to allow input to be edited as it is entered. Only when the entire input is entered and edited will it be transmitted to the host computer. When your terminal is on the west coast talking to a computer on the east coast, the savings in communications costs can be significant. Also, smart terminals provide consistent, fast response because they are dedicated to one user, whereas the host computer may be serving many users.

The disadvantage of smart terminals is their cost and the requirement that they be programmed. They often must be programmed in their own esoteric language, which must be learned by each new programmer, supported by a primitive operating system. By contrast, all the programming for a dumb terminal is done on the host computer, which generally has standard languages, many programming aids, and an extensive operating system.

Response

An important difference between batch and on-line systems is the response time. With a batch system, where you may have four hour turnaround, a half hour difference does not mean much. But the faster the turnaround, the more annoying are the delays. If you are sitting at a typewriter and hit the return key, your level of impatience diminishes to about two seconds, and beyond 15 seconds you begin to get frustrated and reach for the telephone. Response time is the single most important human consideration in on-line systems. The lower limit is about 30 milliseconds, the flicker rate of the human eye—the rate at which the human eye can distinguish discrete images. The faster the turnaround, the less our patience. When you are getting one second response from a terminal, a five second response is excruciating.

Availability

A more subtle problem is the impact of on-line usage on the system availability. With batch systems the system can crash, and only after a while will you notice the slower turnaround time. But with an on-line system the telephone will be ringing off the wall in the computer room 10 seconds after the system crashes. Every user that is logged on will be immediately affected by the problem. Hardware and software problems are much more noticeable and annoying for on-line users than for batch users. The on-line user is sensitive to any change in response, and on-line users can often detect a system crash before the computer operators.

System availability is immensely more demanding with on-line systems than with batch systems. And the further away the users are, the worse it becomes. An installation that does system testing from 5 to 8 A.M. on the west coast would have to change its schedule if on-line users on the east coast are brought onto the system, or it would be unavailable for them from 8 to 11 A.M.

The computer hardware and software are more sophisticated for on-line systems. The hardware is usually not a problem for a programmer in a batch system, but it is a problem for the on-line user. If the computer fails in a batch system, you as a programmer do not have to call the customer engineers and try to convince them that there is something wrong. But when you have a terminal at a remote location, you may have to do just that. And it is even worse than this because of the most terrible of all things—multiple vendors.

One vender may supply the terminal, another vendor the modem, and a third the communication lines. At the other end there is another modem, a message processor, and then the host computer. Thus there may be six vendors. Now suppose that you press the LOGON button on your terminal and nothing happens. Whom do you call? The goal of each vendor is, of course, to pass the problem on to someone else. It is up to you to isolate the trouble, to convince the proper vendor that it is his problem, and to get the vendor to make the repair. The end result can be some of the most frustrating days you are likely to have in your career.

Remoteness

An important consideration in on-line computing is its remoteness. The terminal may be located hundreds of miles from its host computer. The terminal users may be completely isolated from any support or expertise. Their entire view of the computer is limited to their typewriter platen or their CRT screen. Because of this remoteness, much more human engineering is needed for on-line systems than for batch systems. On-line users need to be kept informed of what is going on, they need to be reassured that their input has been received, and they need to be protected against their actions damaging themselves or the system.

Skill

Another difference between on-line and batch users is the physical skill required. Almost anyone can wield a pencil and fill out a computer input form. But on-line terminals have keyboards, and not everyone is an excellent typist. It is sad to see a highly educated user sitting at a sophisticated terminal connected to a multimillion dollar computer using the hunt and peck technique to enter input. If you are a programmer, you had better learn to type well.

Background

A further difference between batch and on-line users is that the users of batch systems are computer programmers. The users of on-line systems may not be. They might know nothing about computers, and they may want to know nothing. They may be unfamiliar with computer terminology, they may distrust computers, and they may not even like computer people.

Design Considerations

Input from a typewriter terminal is somewhat different than that of a CRT terminal because the user must respond to each individual request. To enter input, you prompt the user with a request and indicate when a response is expected.

ENTER YOUR EMPLOYEE ID: _

Your design needs to take into consideration the speed of the terminal. No one wants to sit and wait for a typewriter to type long sentences, especially when the system is used daily by the same people. You should be as terse as comprehensible. The previous input request is probably too long. It would be better as:

ID: _

Use abbreviations and whatever else can keep down the amount that must be typed. Some systems provide both a short and a long form and allow the user to select which is wanted. Neophites would select the long form until they learn the system well enough to use the short form. This sounds great, but it is too expensive to program for most applications. Another method is to provide a HELP button that when pressed gives an explanation of the current request. But again this is expensive to program. Too many options often confuse. You are probably better to stick with a single terse form and provide any necessary elaboration in a user manual. People catch on to short forms and abbreviations so quickly that it is not worth a great deal of effort to provide alternatives.

Since CRT terminals are faster than typewriter terminals, you need not be so terse. But do not give the user more than is needed because it clutters up the screen and takes time to read. Whatever terminal you use, you need to minimize the amount of information that the users must enter. Even if they have skill in typing, they probably do not enjoy it. There are several ways of minimizing what the user must enter. The first is to allow abbreviations, such as Y for yes and N for no. You can also phrase questions so that the user can answer yes or no:

MARRIED (Y OR N)? _

With abbreviations, you can list the possible responses to prompt the user.

MARITAL STATUS (M S D W C): _

    The user might have to refer to the user manual once to learn that the options are Married, Single, Divorced, Widowed, or Cohabiting. Abbreviations also have the advantage that they reduce spelling or typing errors. If you look at only the first character of a yes or no answer, you can accept a response of YES, YUP, YEA, or YESSAH.

    It is nice for a system to allow spelling variation, but the application programs you write probably will not merit the effort required to do this. You are better off to permit a single, short, unambiguous response. If nothing else, it makes the user manual easier to write because you do not have to describe the many options.

    Another way to reduce input information is to provide defaults. The user then only has to change the default if it is inappropriate:

NUMBER OF DEPENDENTS: 1

    A third way to reduce input is to provide a menu from which the user selects. On a typewriter terminal you list the options and adopt some convention such as a carriage return to denote a null response. The users then respond to each menu item with a carriage return until the one comes up that is wanted, and then they hit the SEND key:

MARITAL STATUS
    SINGLE [cr]
    MARRIED [cr]
    DIVORCED [cr]
    WIDOWED [cr]
    COHABITING [send]

    In writing the user manual, you will want to provide examples to guide the user. Adopt a convention to indicate what the system types and what the user types. You might enclose the user response in brackets [], underline, or use lowercase.

    On a CRT terminal you can display all options of the menu on the screen and let the user position the cursor under the one wanted. Menus are better with CRTs because CRTs allow the user to see all the menu items before making a selection.

    In designing the input, you must make provision for the user to change what has been entered. This is especially a problem for typewriter terminals. With CRT terminals the user responds to a page of queries before hitting a SEND key. But with a typewriter terminal the user must respond to each query as it occurs. One way to allow the user to change what has already been entered is to provide a backup function. You might preempt a function key on the terminal to back the system up to the previous query. By hitting the backup key repetitively, the users can work their way back to change any query. When they space forward again, their previous responses can become defaults.

Error messages should also be short and descriptive. Often you do not need a great deal of information. One of the first conversational systems for use by nonprogrammers had only one response for syntax errors: a simple "EH?." Since the syntax was simple and a typical line had less than 10 characters, users could easily find the error.

On-line systems benefit from some personality. The system should be attentive, polite, sympathetic, and forgiving. Do not make the user work day in and out with an obnoxious on-line system. Some terminals have an audio response, generally a small buzzer or whistle. These can be annoying, especially when they are used to announce an error. Imagine yourself in a crowded terminal room in which your terminal gives a blast of a buzzer every time you make an error.

On-line users need a constant response time. Constant response is even more important than fast response. If a system gives a constant two second response, this is acceptable. But if it gives a half second response during light periods and a two second response during heavy periods, this is annoying. If a system is serving many users, you may want to give some minimum response time, even though the system could respond faster when it is unloaded, in order to provide a constant response.

In designing an on-line system you have an obligation to keep the user informed of what is happening. Do not leave the user dangling. If the on-line system is going to take some minutes to retrieve a file, let the user know this:

FILE: <u>cost</u>
TAKE A BREAK. I'LL BE A FEW MINUTES.

Always give the user some indication that the input has been received when it is sent. A carriage return, a movement of the cursor, or typing a message can do this. If the user types in some information and sends it to the computer and there is no immediate response, frustration sets in.

You must protect users from their actions. For example, you might have a command to delete a file with the following query:

DELETE FILE (Y OR N)? _

It is easy to respond incorrectly to such a request, especially in the conversational mode when things are moving fast. If the user types YES when NO is meant, the file is lost. When there is the possibility for doing damage such as this, you might request confirmation:

ARE YOU SURE? (Y OR N)? _

You might also rephrase the original query to ask for file name:

DELETE FILE (GIVE NAME): _

THIRTEEN

Functional Documentation

Documentation ranks in excitement just below a trip to the dentist. Not only is documentation dull, it also leads to hypocrisy. Nothing else in computing gets so much lip service with so little delivered value.

DOCUMENTATION OVERVIEW

To understand some of the problems with documentation, let us look at a far from unusual case history of a system. When the schedule is made out for the design and implementation of the system, a large slice of time is allocated for the documentation as the last step in the schedule. But as the system development lags behind schedule, this time is preempted for system testing. When the system is finally implemented, the customer has a working system and does not want to pay extra for documentation, and the programmer is anxious to move on to a new project. The result is that the programmer slaps a few sloppy flowcharts together, piles in some record and report layout forms, writes a turgid narrative, encloses it in nice plastic sheets, and considers it a job well done.

As time goes by and the system actually works, the programmer is promoted for this remarkable accomplishment. Some of the documentation remains in the programmer's desk, some is put in a program library, and some gets lost in the shuffle. An unfortunate programmer, you for example, is assigned to maintain the system. At first you try to keep the documentation up to date, but you find that much of it is inaccurate, that you actually use little of it, and soon you abandon the effort. By the time the second generation maintenance programmer is assigned to the system, about all that remains of value is the source listing.

From this scenario, several things emerge. If documentation is made a separate effort at the end of a project, it probably will not be done or will be of poor quality. It is also apparent that it is easy for documentation to get out of date. Finally, it proves that you can, if you must, get by without much documentation.

So if we can get by without much documentation, why do it? What do we actually need? And what constitutes good documentation? Good questions that we should answer.

The Use of Documentation

First, let us examine the reasons for documenting. Among these are:

- To express the design of a system, permit its evaluation, and obtain agreement on what the system is to do.
- To implement a system, telling how to write the programs.
- To prepare any necessary inputs, to understand and use the output, and to answer questions about the system.
- To run the job. To know what files are required, how to submit jobs, and how to verify and distribute the output.
- To maintain, change, extend, or resurrect a program.

These are the traditional reasons. There are several others that may come into play:

- To provide continuity in the event that programmers are reassigned, terminate, or abscound.
- To evaluate the programmer and to provide a quality control function.
- To interface to other systems, to understand the state of files, and to know what they contain and how they came to contain the information.
- To publicize a program of interest to others.
- To appraise your management of the fantastic work you are doing.

The Users of Documentation

From these uses of documentation it is evident that there are several audiences. This is important to recognize because the documentation must be directed toward its intended audience if it is to be effective. The audiences for documentation are:

- Those designing and reviewing the system.
- Those implementing the programs.
- The end users.
- Those running the system.

- Those maintaining the system.
- Management.

Given the need for documentation and its users, several types of documentation emerge. Most systems should have these types of documentation, although not necessarily as separate items:

- Design documentation. The audience is a programmer or analyst and possibly the customer.
- Implementation documentation. (Also termed program specifications.) The audience is a programmer.
- User documentation. The audience is the end user of the system who may or may not be a programmer. If the audience is a programmer, the user documentation is often combined with the programmer documentation.
- Programmer documentation. The audience is a programmer, and the documentation is used to maintain and change the system.
- Run documentation. The audience can be an operator, a programmer, and end user, or a production control group.

Approaches to Documentation

There are two approaches to documentation. The first is very formal and rigid; all forms and procedures are exactly spelled out in great detail. The programmer is given little latitude in documenting. Given human nature, this approach to documentation must be firmly enforced, preferably by a former prison commandant with a penchant for whips.

As a rule, only large projects and organizations have the resources to impose and enforce strict documentation standards. If you are working in this environment, documentation will not be a problem. You will do as you are told.

But in most organizations there are some loose documentation guidelines, several discarded attempts at rigid documentation, some good intentions, but the quality and quantity of documentation depends on the programmer's commitment and ability.

Recognizing Good Documentation

One of the problems in documentation is to recognize what good documentation is. The reason most attempts at rigid documentation fail is that they concentrate on form and not substance, and they ask for too much. And so they are ignored. Let us examine the attributes that documentation should have.

1   Documentation should be accessible. Documentation is wasted if you cannot find it when you need it, or if you do not know that it exists. Besides, misplaced documentation is not kept current. In any system there should be a single place where all the documentation for that system is kept. You ought to be able to pick it up and know that you have all the documentation pertaining to that system. This does not sound like much, but it is an important first step in documentation.

2   Documentation should be accurate. This is the most difficult part of documentation. Many systems have been delivered with accurate documentation which is then not kept up to date and soon becomes worthless. The fact is, forms of documentation that are difficult to keep up to date are bad. Program flowcharts are the worst. Minor program changes may require redrawing several flowcharts, and consequently, if there are current flowcharts when a system is completed, they may soon become obsolete. The traditional report and record layout sheets likewise are difficult to change.

3   The documentation should provide what is needed. Not every program deserves the same documentation effort. A one shot program to reformat a file requires little documentation; a production system within a company deserves more documentation; and a program product for a community of users requires even more documentation. The more a program is used and the wider its audience, the more elaborate the documentation needs to be. Documentation is a form of communication, and you must put more effort into communicating to a wider audience. There is also a marginal utility to documentation. For each system there is a level of documentation beyond which it is not economical to prepare more documentation.

   Aim the documentation toward the intended user. Do not use programmer jargon in a user manual. The end users, the programmers, and those who run the program may all have different technical backgrounds and interests. The end user may be an accountant who does not see the preparation of input or the interpretation of output as a career.

4   The documentation should be economical. Programmers do not envision documenting as their life's work, and customers do not want to pay excessive amounts for documentation. We ought to be able to create and maintain documentation with reasonable effort. Among the techniques for making documentation economical are the following:

   •   Eliminate redundancy. There is a saying that a person with one watch always knows the time, but a person with two watches is always unsure. Duplicate documentation is expensive to create and maintain, and inevitably the duplicates do not agree, leaving the reader to guess which is correct. A common example is preparing file layout sheets for each program using a file, rather than creating a single file description to be used by all programs.

- Eliminate items not used. If flowcharts are not used, they might as well not have been prepared. Documentation that is not used but only revised to be kept current should be discarded. If you are not going to use it, why keep it up to date?

- Use forms. Too many forms are a pain, but a few well chosen forms can save effort. Forms are useful because they save you having to write the same headings over and over, and they prompt you on the information that is needed.

- Use source for documentation. Source listings can replace flowcharts, sample reports can replace report layout sheets, and COBOL record descriptions can replace record layout sheets. The JCL listing tells the memory requested, the I/O devices needed, and the estimated CPU time. The accounting information from a run indicates in many systems the actual memory used, the actual CPU time, the elapsed run time, and on some systems the I/O count for each file. Source as documentation not only saves effort in creating it, but also ensures that the documentation is kept current.

- Begin the documentation early. The documentation should drive the programming rather than being done after the fact. Thus the overview documentation should be done at the beginning, and the detailed documentation consisting of source listings, record descriptions, and sample reports are an inherent part of the programming process. At the end of the project, about all that remains to prepare is an inventory of the documentation.

- Label things. Name and label the files, records, programs, reports, tables, JCL procedures, and systems wherever they appear. The name should uniquely identify the item.

- Date each item. The date may be the only way a reader has of knowing how current the documentation is.

- Be consistent. Use consistent terminology, names, and notations in the documentation. This saves the effort of thinking up names for items already named, and it also saves the reader effort. Do not let your documentation be like a Russian novel in which every character has several names, the use of which depends on the people speaking.

- Develop documentation that is easy to change. Double space written documentation and use penciled notations to clarify or correct documentation. A good on-line text editor is invaluable for creating and maintaining source listings, record descriptions, and written documentation. The reason is that text editors excel at revising, and a major problem in documentation is keeping it current. If a good text editor is available, familiarize yourself with it and use it to maintain your documentation.

With this as background, we can move on to some specific techniques for documentation. We concentrate on documentation that you will likely be preparing during your first years in programming: user, programmer, and run documentation.

USER DOCUMENTATION

User documentation often takes the form of a manual. The most important consideration is to identify the audience and direct the manual to them. Try to understand what they will need and want to know, provide it, and stop there. The best example is a cookbook. The cookbook does not tell you how to grow the ingredients, where to buy your pots and pans, or what to do if you cannot light the stove. It simply tells you how to prepare the dish. You cannot cover everything in the user manual. Concentrate on the "how to" questions, not the "what if" questions. Do not overwrite. The "lo and behold" writers are the worst. They can never say "lo" without adding "behold" when either would suffice.

Start writing the user manual early. This forces you to view the system from the user's point of view. The result is often a better understanding of the system in its intended environment. Another way to get the point of view of the users is to enlist their help in writing the manual.

Contents of User Manual

The user manual can be anything from a simple memo for a small program, all the way up to a formal publication. You might include error descriptions, exceptions, restrictions, audit trails, and schedules. Whether these items belong in the user manual or in the program or run documentation depends upon who will be interested in them. The following items will be in most user manuals.

Overview   Describe how to use the manual. Place the reader in perspective by briefly relating the purpose of the system and what can be obtained from it. Tell what must be done to use the system. Describe any concepts that form a key part of the system.

System Flow   Show the organization or steps within the system. Do not feel restricted to a flowchart; other graphical or pictorial forms may convey the information better. The users will probably not care how the computer portion of the system works, and so it may appear as a single box. But the users will care how they interface to the system. Choose a notation that allows the users to quickly grasp the processes. Usually the system flow will show the flow of documents through the system. Figure 22 contains an example of a system flow diagram. Be a little careful in your diagrams because some people resent being depicted by stick figures. You may also run into problems if the stick figures depict the wrong gender.

Input Descriptions   Describe how to prepare the inputs and what is to be done with them.

Output Descriptions   Describe the output reports in enough detail to be understood without reference to other sources. Include annotated sample reports if necessary.

Error Messages   If the error messages themselves are not sufficiently descriptive, further describe them in the user manual. Often a listing of all error messages that can be encountered is helpful.

Procedures   The user manual usually contains step-by-step procedures. Organize the procedures in the sequence in which they must be performed and make each step description self-contained. It is distracting to flip back and forth when following instructions. And remember that people rarely read completely through a set of procedures before they begin.

Debug the procedures. It quickly becomes obvious when a writer has never used the procedures being described, and this does not generate warm feelings. Write the procedures while you are performing them to ensure that they work, that they are in the proper sequence, and that you have not left any out. Enlist the aid of the user to critique the procedures so that they are understandable to their intended audience.

Examples   Use lots of examples, but keep them short and simple. Long, involved examples will bore the reader. The adroit use of examples can significantly reduce the amount of explaining you must do.

Narrative   Stick to the point. Do not distract the readers with long discussions of things of which they have no interest. Manuals are not read for pleasure, but to find out how to do something.

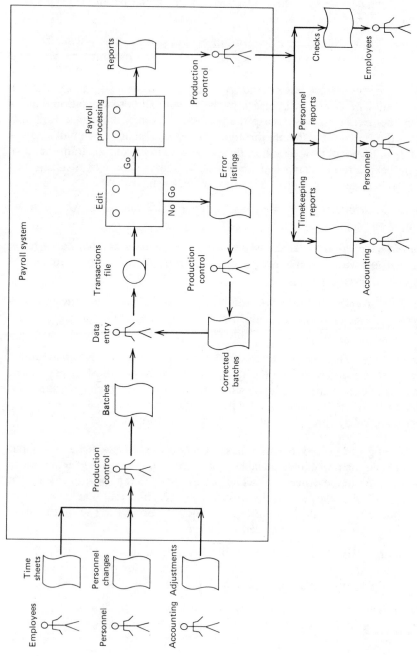

Figure 22 System flow diagram.

Writing the Manual

Write simply, concisely, and clearly. Keep away from computer jargon if the reader is not a programmer. Three things can happen with unfamiliar technical jargon, all bad:

1 The reader may not understand.
2 The reader may understand something different from what you want.
3 The reader may understand exactly what you meant and conclude that he knows as much about a technical subject as you.

Keep the terminology and notations simple. Do not invent new terminology that needs to be defined. The user is interested in using the system, not in vocabulary building. If you must use unfamiliar terms, do not define them all at the beginning. You will put the reader to sleep. Define each new term where it is first used. If you want to provide a glossary, do so, but put it at the back and still define the new terms where they first appear. Glossaries are usually a waste of time because no one reads them.

As an example of how not to communicate with the user, a programmer writing an interactive terminal system inserted a "HELP" command as an aid to the user to explain the other commands. Hitting the "HELP" button yielded a page of explanation—in Backus normal form (BNF). The programmer never considered that the engineers, accountants, and managers would not want to leap up from their terminals and learn the BNF metalanguage used to specify ALGOL. Nor did the programmer consider the contradiction that asking for help required learning a whole metalanguage.

PROGRAMMER DOCUMENTATION

Programmer documentation has two parts. The first part describes the system as a whole, including the components, their relationships, and all the files. The second part describes the individual programs that make up the system. Files are external to programs and should be documented as part of the overall system documentation. Then they need to be documented only once. Much of the program documentation evolves directly from the design and implementation documentation, and you need only ensure that it is current.

Keep the system documentation with the program documentation. In fact, keep all the documentation together. A three ring binder is a convenient container for documentation. Most installations will have some form of library for storing listings, documentation, test decks, and perhaps source decks, although more often the source decks will be kept on direct-access storage.

System Documentation

System documentation consists of the following items.

Inventory   Prepare an inventory of the materials that exist for the system and where they are located. The inventory might include source listings, source decks, test materials, user manuals, run documentation, file and record descriptions, and whatever else is extant for the system. Generally one sheet as the first page of the documentation will do. The inventory makes the materials accessible to the programmer by telling what exists and where it is kept. Figure 23 contains a sample inventory.

Abstract   Prepare an abstract of the system describing what it does. The abstract familiarizes the reader with the system.

System Flow   Prepare a system flowchart that shows the major components of the system. The system flowchart shows which programs are in the system and the sequence in which they are executed. It also shows where files are created, updated, and discarded.

The best tool for showing the system flow is a flowchart in which each program is represented as a single box. Show all the input files, output files, and note where they are created, updated, and discarded. Show any sorts and note the sort order. Label each program and file so that they can be easily identified. The flow should move from the top of the page to the bottom. If the programs do not all fit on a page, continue in sequence on the following page. If you need to see the entire flow, tape the sheets together and tack them on a wall.

Show all the input and output files separately for each program. By making each program stand by itself with its input and output files, you can cut and paste to rearrange the flowchart if the order of execution is changed. Do not try to tie files together in the system flow. If the same file is used a few steps later, do not connect it with a line. This clutters up the flowchart and makes it difficult to maintain. Tie files together by their names.

The system flow is closely related to the JCL. In fact, a commented listing of the JCL can serve as the system flow for minor systems. For larger systems a system flow diagram such as that shown in Figure 24 might be used.

Naming Conventions   Specify the data set naming conventions, file naming conventions, and program naming conventions. Any system will benefit

SYSTEM INVENTORY

SYSTEM NAME: MRCA (MACHINE RESOURCES COST ACCOUNTING)

ACCOUNT NUMBER: 9304

  I. SOURCE DECKS (on USER50 pack)
      PROGRAMS: MONTHLY (Monthly runs)
                      QUARTER (quarterly runs)
                      ANNUAL   (annual runs)
      SUBROUTINES: AMT
                      DATE
                      READTB

  II. SOURCE LISTINGS (in DP library)
      MRCA binder. Listing for each source deck.

 III. TEST JCL (on USER50 pack)
      JCL.TEST.MONTHLY tests MONTHLY.
      JCL.TEST.QUARTER tests QUARTER.
      JCL.TEST.ANNUAL tests ANNUAL.

 IV. TEST JCL RESULTS (in DP library)
      MRCA binder. Results of above test JCL.

  V. PROGRAMMER DOCUMENTATION (in DP library)
      MRCA three-ring binder: Correspondence
                              System flowchart
                              File layouts
                              Overall descriptions
                              Detailed documentation
                              Unique characteristics

 VI. PRODUCTION CONTROL DOCUMENTATION (in PC library)
      CP.PA binder: System description
                     Program description
                     Run schedule
                     JCL listings
                     Input forms and preparation
                     Tape log
                     Output distribution instructions

VII. USER MANUAL (in DP library)
      MRCA USERS MANUAL binder: Overview
                                  System flow
                                  Input forms
                                  Output reports
                                  Error messages

Figure 23   Sample system inventory.

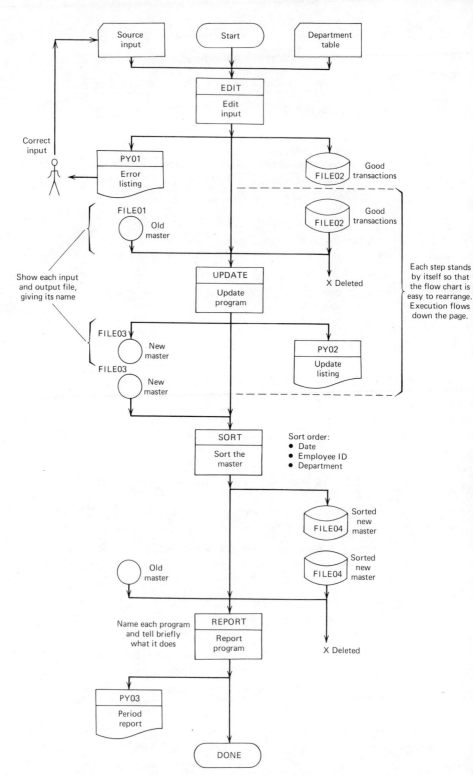

Figure 24 System flowchart.

from consistent naming conventions. Keep in mind, however, that elaborate naming conventions usually break down. For example, if you use the data name to indicate the file retention, what do you do if you change the file retention—rename the files? Choose names that will not have to be changed.

Execution Aids Document any utility programs such as those that initialize, dump, or reformat files. Tell how to use them and what purpose they serve.

Audit Trail If the system contains an audit trail that allows transactions to be traced through the system, explain it to the reader.

JCL Listings of JCL should be treated and maintained the same as source listings. Include the JCL for testing and special runs.

Change Procedures Some control must be exercised over change, and the procedures belong in the system overview.

File and Record Documentation

The file and record documentation is actually a part of the system documentation, although it is described separately here. Document each file and record. This is important because you cannot tell what the data is if it is not documented. You can read a program and understand the computations done on the data, but unless you understand the data, the program will have little meaning.

File Documentation Document each file with the following information:

- File name
- File organization
- Record length
- Blocksize (if this may change, refer the reader to the JCL creating the file)
- Storage medium
- Rotation and retention of files

COBOL requires that a file description (FD) be coded for each file, and the FD contains much of this information. Consequently the FD can be used to document the file by adding necessary comments. Place the FD in a COPY library to save programming effort and enforce consistency. Figure 25 contains a sample file description.

You may want to prepare a cross-reference listing of the files. The listing should contain the name of the program creating the file, the program names that update the file, and the program names that read or access the

```
****          MEMBER COPY (PAYMFD)
*FD   PAYM-FILE
      RECORDING MODE IS F
      RECORD CONTAINS 97 CHARACTERS
      BLOCK CONTAINS 1940 CHARACTERS
      LABEL RECORDS STANDARD
      DATA RECORDS ARE PAYM-REC.
  01  PAYM-REC.
      05  FILLER           PIC X.
      05  PAYM-KEY         PIC X(18).
      05  FILLER           PIC X(78).
```

Figure 25   Sample file description.

file. The cross-reference listing is especially useful in determining the programs affected when a file is changed. But the problem with a cross-reference listing is the effort to maintain it. The system flow diagram contains the same information, although it takes a little more time to dig it out. Do not prepare cross-reference listings if experience tells you that they will not be kept current.

Record Documentation   The record documentation is usually combined with the file documentation. However, it may be separate where a file contains several record formats or a record is contained in several files. The record documentation should contain the following information:

- Record format
- Field names
- Format of each field
- Descriptions of each field's contents

The amount of description for each field depends upon the complexity and importance of the system. For an elaborate data base system there might be a page of description for each data item in a record. But usually you will need much less.

Record layout sheets are often used for record descriptions, but they are poor. There is not enough room to name the data items, tell their format, and adequately describe them. Record layout sheets are also difficult to change. If a field must be expanded, all the fields following it in the record must be moved down in the layout sheet.

A better way to describe records in COBOL is to use the record descriptions themselves to document the records. These descriptions already name each field in the record and specify its format. You can complete the documentation by adding comments to describe the data fields. Place the file description in a COBOL COPY library so that it need be coded only once for all programs using the file, and all programs are forced to use the same data names. This automatically puts the record documentation in the source listing of each program using the file. You make the documentation drive the programming rather than allowing it to be a haphazard afterthought.

This technique also makes it easy to keep the record documentation up to date. When the file is changed, the record descriptions must be changed, and the documentation in the form of comments is right there to be changed too.

In documenting the record descriptions with comments, place them on the right side of the page so that they do not distract from the data descriptions. Align all the PIC clauses and start each comment in the same column position for readability. The comments should include a description of each data item. For flags and codes, tell the meaning of values within the item as shown in the following example:

```
05   FLSA        PIC X.
*                            EXEMPTION CODE
*                              E—EXEMPT
*                              N—NONEXEMPT
05   STATUS      PIC X.
*                            MARITAL STATUS
*                              M—MARRIED
*                              S—SINGLE
```

The one item of information contained in record layout sheets which is not provided by documenting the record descriptions with comments is the relative byte position of each field. You will need to know this to determine the record length, to use an external sort, and to read an unformatted file dump. Some compilers list the relative byte position of each field in the compilation listing, and if so, this solves the problem. But if not, you can add this information as comments. Place the relative byte positions in columns 73 to 80 of the data description. Unfortunately, if you expand or insert a field, this will change the relative byte position of all the following fields in the record, and you will have to change the comments. Nonetheless this is still easier than redrawing a record layout sheet.

In naming the data items within a record, you might give the level 01 item a short name and append this name to all items within the record so that whenever the items are used in the program, it will be apparent from which record they come. Figure 26 contains an example of a COBOL record description that also serves to document the record.

```
****        MEMBER COPY(PAY)
****        PAY IS THE MASTER PAYROLL FILE.
****        RECORD LENGTH IS 31 BYTES.
****        LAST UPDATED ON 7/4/1985 BY J.JONES.
  01  PAY.
      05  PAY-NAME.
*                             NAME OF PERSON
          10  PAY-NAME-LAST    PIC X(12).                      1.
          10  PAY-NAME-FIRST   PIC X(12).                     13.
          10  PAY-NAME-INITIAL PIC X.                         25.
*                             MIDDLE INITIAL.
      05  PAY-CODE             PIC X.                         26.
*                             TYPE OF PAY.
*                             H – HOURLY
*                             S – SALARIED
      05  PAY-SALARY           PIC S999V99.                   27.
*                             HOURLY RATE
```

Figure 26   Sample COBOL record description.

Program Documentation

Program documentation, the most detailed type of documentation, is used
to answer questions, correct errors, and make changes. Fortunately much
of the documentation is automatically done during the process of writing
the program, of which the source listing is the most important. Most maintenance programmers go right to the source listing anyway, ignoring other
documentation, because they know from sad experience that this is about
all they can trust. And they need to go to the source listing anyway to make
changes and correct errors.

The narrative at the beginning of the program can give the readers
enough of an overview in a few sentences to prepare them to read the listing.
Do not cross-reference the narrative into the program because it is unlikely
to be maintained. Leave cross-referencing to the compiler.

Many installations use a form for program documentation, such as the
example shown in Figure 27. By itself, such a form does not contain much
of value, but it does serve an important purpose. It provides a sheet of paper
that can be filed with the system documentation, and any other written
documentation pertaining to the program can be filed behind this sheet.
These might include structured diagrams, pseudocode, decision tables, and
memos. The fact that such a form helps to organize the documentation is
often enough to justify its use. Program documentation should also consist of the following:

Narrative   Briefly describe the inputs to the program, the processing, and
the outputs, and include them as comments in the IDENTIFICATION

PROGRAM DESCRIPTION

SYSTEM NAME: _____

SYSTEM ID: _____

DATE: _____

PROGRAM NAME: _____

PROGRAM ID: _____

INPUT: _____

_____

_____

PROCESSING: _____

_____

_____

OUTPUT: _____

_____

_____

NOTES: _____

_____

_____

Figure 27 Sample program documentation form.

DIVISION of the COBOL program. Describe any special algorithms, equations, or methods not described elsewhere. Tell the readers what they are likely to want to know, and make it easy for them to get any additional detail from the source listing.

Input Descriptions Include these only if they are not given in a user manual.

Output Descriptions Anyone modifying the program will need to know what the reports look like. Reports may also be described in the user manual, but do include them as a part of the program documentation. Rather than laying out the report on a columnar report layout sheet, collect a printed sample of the report. A form may also be handy to help document a report, giving such information as estimated pages, distribution, the summarization done, and the source of the data.

Test Materials Include the test materials with the documentation and maintain them along with the program.

Error Descriptions   As a rule, error messages directed to the programmer do not need additional explanation. They should be made sufficiently descriptive that no secondary reference is required. But they are awfully nice to have listed because they help in understanding the program.

Exceptions   Exceptions are confusing because they make no sense unless you understand the reason for the exception. Clearly note each exception and why it is an exception.

Restrictions   Restrictions limit the scope of what can be done with the program. Make sure that the reader's attention is drawn to the restrictions.

Required Resources   The memory size, disk, and tape needed, and other hardware resources required are usually specified in the JCL. If not, include them in the program documentation.

Source Listing   The source listing is also an important documentation item. Make sure that someone can find the current copy and know that it is current. The following techniques will aid in making the source listing serve as documentation.

- Page ejects. Separate major sections of code with page ejects. Use blank lines to separate smaller units of code.
- Comments. Let the statements show what the program does, and use comments to tell why it is doing it. Comment exceptions, restrictions, data, flags, and coding schemes. Set the comments off with rows of asterisks or indent the comment to the right so that it does not obscure the code.

```
**** SET THE COMMENT OFF WITH ASTERISKS TO
**** HIGHLIGHT IT AND ENSURE THAT IT IS NOT
**** CONFUSED WITH THE LANGUAGE STATEMENTS.
*                             OR START THE
*                             COMMENTS IN THE
*                             RIGHT SIDE OF
*                             THE PAGE SO THAT
*                             THEY DO NOT
*                             OBSCURE THE
*                             LANGUAGE
*                             STATEMENTS.
```

- Do not write on the listing. Your writing will disappear with the next compilation. Also, it is disconcerting to pick up a listing with changes penciled in. Did someone intend these changes to be made the next time the program is recompiled, or are these changes that have already been made, but for which a new listing has not been filed?

- Always request a cross-reference listing of data items and paragraph names from the compiler.
- Make sure that the reader can quickly tell which files are input and which are output.
- Include the program's author and the date it was written.
- Record program changes to a production program in the source listing. In the narrative section of the program note the date, the person making the change, and the change made. Assign a version number to each modified program placed in production and include the version number in the source listing:

```
**** 7/4/1985  VERSION PPPC0114 CHANGE MADE BY J. JONES
**** 1. THE CONDITION CODE WAS CHANGED FROM A
                                  VALUE OF 16 TO 14.
**** 2. THE SEARCH FOR THE DEPARTMENT NUMBER WAS
            CHANGED FROM SEQUENTIAL TO BINARY.
```

- Code a single sentence per line, align the code to show the hierarchy, use parentheses to indicate the order of operations, and select short, descriptive data names.

```
A10-PROCESS-PAY-MASTER.
*                       PERHAPS USE ALPHA-
*                       NUMERIC PREFIX TO
*                       INDICATE RELATIVE
*                       SEQUENCE OF PARAGRAPH
*                       NAMES IN LISTING.
    OPEN INPUT PAY-MASTER-OLD,
              PAY-TRANS,
              PAY-TIMESHEETS.
    IF ((EMP-AGE = 7) AND (EMP-IQ = 100))
        THEN MOVE MIN-WAGE TO EMP-SALARY
        ELSE IF (EMP-AGE = 100) OR
              ((EMP-AGE = 30) and (EMP-IQ = 160))
              THEN MOVE ZEROS TO EMP-SALARY.
```

- Make clear the beginning and ending of any logical unit of code. If a paragraph is performed, indicate that execution does not continue into the next paragraph.

A10-PARAGRAPH.
        SEVERAL STATEMENTS.
**** EXIT

- Maintain the integrity of the program structure and make it apparent by using PERFORMs. A structure such as:

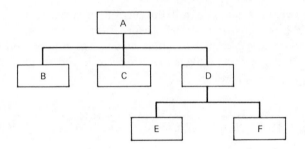

becomes:

A.
        PERFORM B.
        PERFORM C.
        PERFORM D.
        STOP RUN.
B.
        SOME STATEMENTS.
**** EXIT
C.
        SOME STATEMENTS.
**** EXIT
D.
        PERFORM E.
        PERFORM F.
**** EXIT
E.
        SOME STATEMENTS.
**** EXIT
F.
        SOME STATEMENTS.
**** EXIT

RUN DOCUMENTATION

Run documentation can range from commented JCL all the way to formal production control procedures. For simple systems, make the JCL carry as much of the burden as possible by commenting it. For complex systems, the run documentation might be formal procedures. Often the run documentation involves several people, such as accountants, data entry, computer operators, and programmers. As a consequence, it often exists as a collection of separate procedures for each person involved in the process.

The following items are often included in the run documentation.

1 **Schedule** The schedule may include the input cutoff, the time for data entry, the time for batch balancing, the computer run times, the output reconciliation time, and the output distribution time. Explain the dependencies in the schedule between the data and the systems. The schedule is often a listing or some graphical form.

2 **Source input** Indicate how to prepare the source input, who prepares it, and what input forms are used. Explain what control information is submitted with the data and what control information must be supplied after the input is received. Give the amount of input to be expected.

3 **Data entry instructions** Describe the keying instructions, including left zeroing, overpunching minus signs, and tab settings for data entry. For on-line input, describe the procedures for entering the data from the terminal.

4 **Files** Describe the master file rotation and file retention. List whatever volume serial numbers are necessary.

5 **Logs** Describe any input, output, run, or tape logs that must be maintained.

6 **Job submission** Tell what JCL to submit, the volumes to mount, and the sequence and dependencies of job submission. Give the expected CPU time, the memory size, the disk space requirements, and the I/O volume. (This information is often described adequately in the JCL.)

7 **Control procedures** Describe how to batch the input, balance it, correct it, and reconcile the output.

8 **Printed output** Tell which reports are printed, the number of pages to expect, how to verify that the output is correct, and how to distribute it.

9 **Errors**   Tell how to correct errors and where to go for help. Describe the restart procedures. Give your telephone number where you can be reached late at night.

10 **Operator instructions**   Provide any operator instructions and on-line messages that might be printed.

FOURTEEN

Maintenance

Few people enjoy maintenance and fewer would elect to do it. We tend to regard being asked to do maintenance with the same enthusiasm an opera singer would have to being asked to sing backup for a rock group. However, maintenance constitutes roughly half of the programming effort today. Consequently, not only will you likely do maintenance, there is a good chance it will constitute a large part of what you do during your first years in computing.

Most installations have procedures for accepting, evaluating, scheduling, and implementing the program changes that constitute maintenance. As a result, you may follow rather than develop many of the maintenance procedures described in this chapter.

WHY MAINTENANCE?

Maintenance comes about for three reasons: to correct errors, to make functional changes, and to make improvements. Errors will invariably occur, and they occur at the most inopportune time and in the most destructive manner. You can always count on a disaster at 3 A.M. the day you are leaving on vacation. Functional changes come about because of the customer's needs. Improvements come about either to reduce run costs or because of your needs. Old programs are like old cars. They sometimes need to be overhauled to keep them running.

There is actually a fourth reason for maintenance—answering questions. Invariably there are new situations, forgotten procedures, unfamiliar features, and general curiosity that result in questions for you to answer. Answering questions is a form of maintenance, even though no changes are made. Questions require that you analyze and learn the system, and it can occupy a significant portion of your time. In software packages it can occupy most of your time.

There is no clear demarcation between development and maintenance. Change, program improvements, error correction, and answering questions occur during development and continue throughout the life of a system. Given the catalytic effect of computer-generated reports, the most active period for change comes immediately after the system goes into production and people begin receiving reports. It generally declines during the life of the system, but then begins to grow again as needs change and problems pile up, until at some point maintenance is frozen while the entire system is redone. This life cycle is illustrated in Figure 28.

The demands of production computing differ from those of development, and they lead to many considerations, some not at all obvious. A production system will exist for a long time, giving the environment time to change. The operating system will change, the compiler will change, the I/O devices will change, and the computer itself will change. The requirements will change, people will change, and the entire organization will change.

Latent errors will come to life. A single run of the system might not encounter a particular error, but when the system is run often, this error will eventually occur. Most systems contain errors that lie dormant until a particular combination of data or events brings them to life. The longer the system's life, the more that can go wrong.

The system must run on schedule. A schedule must be prepared, input must be coordinated, and conditions that would affect the schedule must be anticipated. Errors require immediate attention, and the pressures are intense. Errors are not serious during development. In fact, you try to make them occur, they occur gracefully during working hours, and you have time allocated to correct them. Users do not gather outside your office to await your solving the error. But when an error occurs during production, it may occur in the dark hours of night, it will impact a schedule, and users will be painfully aware of any delays. "Have you got it fixed yet?" replaces "Hello" as the standard salutation.

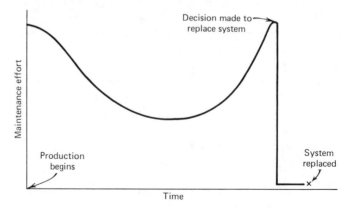

Figure 28   System maintenance life cycle.

Information is retained. This is an enormously complicating factor because errors are cumulative. When an error introduces bad data in a file, correcting the program does not correct the data; the file must be purged of the bad data. Also, other programs will be affected if they read the file with the bad data. Bad data can contaminate an entire system.

Someone else will run the program. Separate people may schedule the runs, submit the job, and check and distribute the output. They must know how to run the job and keep track of files. They must also be able to determine if the system ran successfully, and they must know what to do if the run is unsuccessful.

Sheer volume will cause problems. The system may run too long, the files may become too large, direct-access files may need to be reorganized, and too much output may be printed. A production system may encounter limitations in memory size, CPU time, elapsed running time, tape and disk capacity, and lines of output. Tables may overflow. You must consider backup and recovery. The volume will tend to grow over time, and this may suddenly cause the program to stop running if the maximum capacity of a resource is exceeded.

And finally, someone else will modify the system. The original programmer may be reassigned or leave the company. Someone else—you—must locate errors and make modifications.

DOING MAINTENANCE

You no doubt have heard about such programming methodologies as structured programming and top-down design. Unfortunately, you will probably not be maintaining programs written with these methodologies. More likely, the programs you maintain will appear to have been written by programmers who felt that anyone's understanding the program would be an invasion of privacy. The documentation will be scanty and of uncertain quality. With luck you will be able to locate a source deck and listing, and in some dark corner gathering dust you may come across a file layout. Anything more than this will be serendipitous.

You may also be maintaining package systems. Maintenance for package systems is similar to maintenance for internally developed systems, although you hope that there will be fewer errors and less need for having to make improvements. The external documentation is usually better, but since the package was developed elsewhere, it will be a bit more of a mystery than an internally developed system.

Change will occur as frequently for package systems as for internally developed systems, and may be easier or more difficult to implement. If the package provides what is needed, the change is often simple. If the package does not provide what is needed, the change can be extremely difficult. A package system will be much larger and more complex than an internally developed system because the package must serve a community of users. Even little changes made to large, complex systems can be enormous tasks. The source listing will be less useful with a package system than with an internally developed system. The package's vendor may provide support and answer questions, but generally this turns out to be less useful than it might appear.

Maintenance for a nonprocedural language such as RPG or MARK IV is similar to that for a procedure language such as COBOL, except that the source listing is of less help. With a nonprocedural language, coding a particular character in a column can give the same result as pages of COBOL statements. However, when you read the source listing, all you may see are some characters coded in columns whereas in COBOL you will see pages of readable statements. Nonprocedural languages tend to be commented even less than COBOL, which is very little indeed. Consequently you must depend more on the external documentation than the source listing.

Taking over a System

This leads us to the steps necessary to do maintenance and to take over the maintenance of a system.

Locate the Materials   Whatever materials exist must be found. Cull out what is obsolete or worthless, and organize what remains.

Document the System   The previous chapter covered documentation. You will need at least the following; whatever is missing you should prepare yourself:

- Table of contents
- Source deck and listings
- File and record descriptions
- Sample reports
- JCL decks and listings
- System flowchart
- User manual or whatever documentation the users have
- Run procedures or whatever exists

Find Out What the System Does   The documentation may be adequate to explain what the system does, but this is unlikely. More often you will have to dig this information out yourself. The users are an important source of information. Talk to those preparing the input forms and collect whatever manuals and forms they use. Find out who receives the output reports, obtain samples, and ask the people how the reports are used.

Another important source of information is the run documentation. Talk to the people who run the system. Not only can they point out problems, but they will know about control cards and special initialization runs. In fact, they will probably know more about the system than anyone if the original programmer is not available. Although they may not know programming, they know what the system does, and with their long experience they can often provide answers to detailed questions which might take days to discover by poring over the program listings.

Verify that the system flowchart is accurate. Check which programs are run, in what order, their frequency, and the input to each program and its output. Make sure that you have identified all the input forms, input files, output files, and reports. Identify all the run parameters and control cards because these are also important in understanding the system. Any initialization runs, reset runs, or special year-end procedures should be noted.

Learn the Internals of the System   This is by far the hardest step. Not only may it be technically difficult, it may also be soporific. Reading documentation and poring over source listings is flat boring. The mean time between your beginning to read the documentation and your head hitting your desk as you fall asleep is about 20 minutes. There are some who can learn a system completely by simply sitting down and studying the documentation, but they are few. Most of us need more motivation than the vague goal of "learning" a system.

The best way to learn a system is to make changes to it. When you must make changes, your work is directed. If you have no changes to make, you might compose a list of questions you feel need answered to enable you to understand the system. Ask what the program structure is, what tables are used, and how the data is transformed from input to output. You might also tidy up the source program, aligning statements, indenting, commenting, and inserting blank lines and page ejects. Have something more solid to go on than just the desire to "learn" the system.

Accept Responsibility for the System   You may end up maintaining a system written by a hyperkinetic cryptographer, but users will be depending upon the system's output. Your responsibility will be to keep it running. Even though run failures are due to the original programmer's mistakes, the users will hold you responsible for all that goes wrong. It is frustrating, but you must accept the responsibility.

Making Planned Changes

Over the life of a system there will be a low-level but constant need for changes. The changes usually originate with the customer, although you may originate your own to make the system more manageable, to eliminate potential errors, or to make the system run more efficiently. Since these changes are planned, you can approach them in an orderly fashion.

Establish Control over Changes   Your installation should have some procedures for controlling change. Procedures are needed because customers can drive you up the wall with requests for change. Customers should be encouraged to put their requests in writing, and there needs to be a means of evaluating the requests and setting priorities. The customers know only what they want done. They need to be informed what it will cost, how long it will take, what undesirable side effects might occur, and where the change fits in your priority list.

Once the change is decided upon, confirm it in writing and give the customer a copy. It is important that you and not the customer write this confirmation. You should do this even if the customer has put the request in writing because the request will likely change as you discuss it with the customer.

The written confirmation gives you the opportunity to tell the customer your interpretation and understanding of the change to be made before making it. This should reduce the number of times the customer will come up to you after you have made a change and say "great, but this is not what I wanted." And when it does occur, you will at least have the satisfaction of knowing that you did your best.

Schedule the Change   You will have a backlog of maintenance tasks whereas each customer may have only a single request for change. This leads to conflicts, and you need to assign priorities to your work and keep the customers informed about when they can expect their requests to be done. You may also want to collect several changes to a system and perform them all at once. At best it is more efficient to collect changes. At worst, one big disaster is better than a series of small ones.

Make the Change   In making the change, you must maintain the integrity of the system. Well-written programs will turn sour if subjected to a barrage of quick and dirty changes. Do the job the way it should be done and be leery of expedients because there is usually a price to pay.

Part of the job in making the change is to debug the specifications. No matter how well you think you understand them, there will be questions that arise during the process of actually making the changes. Resolve them, involving the customers if necessary. Then get the understanding in writing. Do not let these last minute interpretations slip through the crack.

Revise the documentation while you make the changes to the program, especially the documentation contained in the source listings. Putting off revisions to the documentation often means that it will not be done.

Desk Check the Changes Most changes have unexpected side effects. Look for them. The side effects might be an increase in memory size, CPU time, or file storage space. A change in data in a file that is used by another program can result in unfortunate side effects. The side effects might also occur within the program where a data item is used as a flag or which controls the iterations in a loop. The possibilities are infinite.

The biggest problem in desk checking is in overcoming a quirk of human nature. Despite there being not a shred of supporting evidence, we all assume that we do not make mistakes. This can defeat desk checking because we are not going to look very hard for errors if we do not believe that they are there. You will notice this phenomenon when you are tracking down the cause of an error in a program. You know an error is present, and you have no problem in concentrating to find it. The result is that you often find several errors in addition to the one causing the problem. It is much easier to find something if you believe it exists. So when you do your desk checking, make yourself believe that there is an error present. You will rarely be disappointed.

There is also another way to accomplish desk checking, with the proper doubting attitude. We all believe that we do not make mistakes, but we have grave doubts that others are so gifted. Let someone else look over the change. Describe what the program does, what you want the change to do, and drop the suggestion that you think you may have introduced an error. They will probably find several.

You may believe that someone else cannot possibly locate program errors in the half hour or so that they are likely to spend. But they can. They will find the errors that you would not think of. They probably will not find complicated logic errors that require an understanding of the entire program, but they will find the unexpected errors.

The process of explaining your changes to someone else forces you to concentrate and to think ahead to try to pick out errors before the listener does. The result is often that the listener sits there completely bored while you suddenly uncover a whole series of problems you had overlooked before.

Having someone else check your code helps in another way reminiscent of the old joke about cleaning the house before the housekeeper arrives so you will not be thought to keep a dirty house. If you know that someone else is going to discover all your dumb mistakes, you will make fewer of them.

The extreme of having someone else look over your program changes is the structured walkthrough in which several people go through a program as a group. The problem with a structured walkthrough is that they are difficult to organize. You will be lucky to get a single person to look over your program, let alone a group. Also a group has limited powers of concentration. Finding errors takes concentration, and groups tend to talk, figit, doze off, digress, and let egos become involved.

Test the Change   Any changes, however trivial, should be tested. The acid test is to use live data, perhaps with a parallel run. When you are correcting errors in a production run, this may be the only way in which you can test. But for scheduled maintenance you need more selective testing, and live data is often inconvenient for this. It may result in prohibitive long running times, or it may not contain data you need to test. Also the live data may change each time you run the program, and for long-term maintenance you need a stable set of test data. The test data may be prepared by extracting it from the live data, by generating it on the computer, perhaps with a test data generator, or by generating it by hand.

You should add to the test data as errors occur, including the data that cause the error, so that the test data is cumulative. Do not discard test data when you correct an error. Keep it, so that when you make another change, you can ensure that you do not reintroduce the error. Over time, your test data should provide a comprehensive set of data that tests all old bugs found in the system, as well as contains representative data.

Along with the test data you should retain the most recent set of reports and run information generated from it. Also keep a copy of the test JCL and listings.

In addition to the test data, you will need to keep a set of files, tables, and control cards. This becomes complex in large systems and may require writing programs to load the test files for debugging. Put some effort in this so that you can quickly switch from a live run to a test run. This reduces some of the inertia in testing.

Verifying test runs leads to the same problem as desk checking. As programmers we assume that if the program did not abnormally terminate, everything must be correct. We tend to glance over the reports, not studying them closely enough to ensure that all is well. Try to break this habit. If you make a parallel run with live data before the change is finally implemented, the users may help you catch errors. They will look at the reports in context, and they often spot subtle errors because the data has meaning to them.

Implement the Change   Once tested, the changed program must be placed in production. You should identify each production program with a name and version number, and then increment the version number each time you change the program in production. Retain the old version, at least for a while, as a backup.

Most installations will have a change form, such as the one shown in

CHANGE FORM

DATE: _____

SYSTEM NAME: _____   PROGRAM NAME: _____

ID: _____   OLD ID: _____

NEW ID: _____

CHANGED BY: _____

DESCRIPTION OF CHANGE: _____

_____

_____

_____

REASON FOR CHANGE: _____

_____

_____

_____

CHECK LIST:

JCL   ☐ _____

FILE DESCRIPTION   ☐ _____

RECORD DESCRIPTION   ☐ _____

TABLE   ☐ _____

REPORT   ☐ _____

PROCEDURES   ☐ _____

CHANGE APPROVED BY: _____

PROGRAM TRANSFER MADE ON (DATE): _____

Figure 29   Sample change form.

Figure 29. If not, devise your own. The change form should identify the change, the program version number associated with it, describe the change, give the reason for the change, and record the data changed. Memos and other notes can be filed behind the form. The change form serves to discipline the change procedure.

Notify those affected by the change. Describe any new procedures or report changes. Memos are a good tool for announcing changes because they can be directed to those involved and they also help document the change and serve notice that the change has been completed.

Complete whatever changes are necessary to the documentation. Revise the user manual. File the new source listing, samples of any revised reports, and any changed file or record description. Revise the JCL, change any run procedures, place the new program version in the production load library, and you are on your way.

Do not plan to be out of town the first time the new version runs in production. Make yourself available in the event something goes wrong. An interesting thing happens when you introduce a revised program into production. Strange, latent errors that have nothing to do with your change will take this time to occur. A user may enter the wrong data or the operator may make a mistake. Whatever, it will occur now. Do not exclude the possibility that something other than your change might be causing the problem.

Maintenance Due to Errors

Errors will, of course, occupy much of your maintenance effort. They generally manifest themselves by either an abnormal termination or bad output. With an abnormal termination, the computer operator or the run group gives you the bad news, often at night when many production jobs are run. With bad output, the user may be the one to discover the error.

Although you have no choice, the abnormal termination, aside from its occurrence at uncivilized hours, is preferable. First, there is unquestionable evidence that something went wrong. And because the program terminates at the point of error, you may immediately know which program statement caused the error. It also means that bad data has not been generated and broadcast into other files. Other than the impact on the schedule, there is less visibility to the error.

When the error results in bad output, it may be some time before it is detected, and by then you can have a real mess on your hands. With bad output, much of the work may be in determining whether there is an error at all. And if the users see the bad output, it reinforces all the cynicism they have about computers.

Identifying Errors   However the error occurs, the first step in the error correction process is to identify it. Often your initial notification of an error comes in a telephone call from a user that goes something like this:

"I just thought you'd like to know your lousy system fouled up again," the user says.

"What do you mean?" you reply with apprehension.

"It's just a bunch of garbage," the user responds.

"What's a bunch of garbage?" you ask.

"This mess that was sitting on my desk," the user says.

"Yes, but what report is it?" you ask.

"Oh, I don't know. I threw the whole thing away when I saw it was bad," the user says.

So there you are. You have no idea what specifically was wrong or even what report it was. In many instances when you pin down the user, it turns out that the report is in fact correct and the user did not understand it. You must get concrete evidence of any error. Anything less wastes your time. Arm waving and vague mutterings do nothing to help you locate an error.

Diagnosing Errors Once you identify the error, the next step is to determine what caused it. This is debugging, a skill that is learned with practice. Undoubtedly you will get plenty of practice.

Debugging has a lot in common with detective work. Watching experienced programmers debug is a little like watching the denouement scene in a detective movie. After having gathered all the suspects together in a room, the detective packs his pipe reflectively while he paces the floor, going over the crime. He suddenly points an accusing finger at the maid, but as quickly discounts her as the culprit because of important shreds of evidence. Eventually, though a process of logic and elimination that in retrospect is perfectly straightforward, he locks the cuffs on the butler as the guilty party. Let us see how this thought process works.

First, we as programmers have a very low threshold of what is an unsolvable problem. We are certain that our programs will run correctly, and when they do not, our reaction is something like: "My program blew up. They must have made some changes to the operating system today."

Our attitude is wrong. In his book, *Zen and the Art of Motorcycle Maintenance*, Robert Pirsig tells about a set of instructions that begin "Assembly of Japanese bicycle requires great peace of mind." The instructions sound irrelevant, but the point is well made that your approach to a problem often determines the outcome. This is especially true of debugging.

You need the correct outlook. You must believe that errors do occur, but that you can solve them. Do not be misled by red herrings, such as suspected problems in the operating system, but quickly focus on what must be causing the error. Do not rationalize the error due to sinister outside forces. Granted, system errors do occur, but the mere fact that a program did not produce the expected results is insufficient proof.

As an example of the debugging process, a programmer had discovered a bug in a program and made the necessary changes to fix it. He then reran the program with the test data, but was surprised to discover the bug still present. His thought process in solving the problem was roughly the following:

1   An error occurred in the original program.

2   Changes were made to the program.

3   The changes should correct the error in step 1 or at least not yield the same results.

4   The program was rerun with the same results as in step 1.

5   The only reasonable explanation for the results in step 4 is that the original program had not been changed.

The programmer then rechecked the compilation listing. Tucked away in the linkage editor step was a missed error message indicating that the step failed because the load library was out of space, resulting in the original program being left intact. The test job then invoked the old program rather than the new one. The programmer was able to solve the problem in a few minutes by determining what was the most reasonable cause and not being distracted by thoughts about the new disk drive added to the computer that week or the new version of the COBOL compiler that was recently installed.

Learn to look for clues, such as the CPU time consumed, the I/O count of the job, and the completion codes or error messages issued by the operating system. Through experience you will soon learn the symptoms of common problems. If a program gives different results in two identical runs, it is almost always because of an uninitialized variable. A memory protection exception is usually due to a bad subscript.

Your first suspect should be the most recent change to the program, if there is one. Often the change works properly, but an unexpected side effect caused by the change will crop up. So even if the symptoms do not apper to be caused by the change, look further.

Interestingly enough, you probably will not need to use abnormal termination dumps often. The dumps take too long to read. They are only marginally useful with higher level languages, and are not needed to solve most errors. But what is needed to solve many problems is for you to read the programming manuals. Many errors originate from a wrong or insufficient understanding of what the language statements actually do.

As a last resort, explain the problem to someone else. They probably will not solve it, but you will in the process of describing the problem to them. It does not really matter to whom you explain the problem. In many instances the other person might as well be a confessional into which you pour your tale of woe. You will often solve the problem about midway through your fourth sentence.

Because production programs have already been debugged, errors tend to fall into three categories. First is capacity. The CPU time of the job, disk storage, or a tape reel may exceed capacity. Fortunately these errors are easy to detect, and their solution does not require program changes. Hardware, operator, or run submission errors are the second main cause. These may be more difficult to detect, but again no program changes are required.

The third main cause of errors is data: incorrect data, unusual data that triggers an error, or a combination of data that cannot be handled by the program. This type of error is often difficult to detect and may require program changes. To solve such errors, you need to know the data involved. The program flow is usually determined by the data, so by knowing the data, you can usually reconstruct the program flow leading up to the error. But how do you locate the data?

The data arrives in the program in an input record and leaves in an output record or a printed report. You may be able to solve the error by examining the printed output. Unfortunately, if the program abnormally terminates, the output buffers may not be flushed, and the last few lines not printed, which is diabolical because these are just the lines you need.

The next step may be to selectively dump the relevant files. The nice thing about file dumps is that they need not be anticipated. They can be done at anytime. File dump utilities or programs should be a standard tool in your repertoire.

Once you locate the data, walk through your program to see how the data will be processed by the program. You act as the computer and keep track of flags, control information, and intermediate data.

If you still have not cracked the problem, you will probably have to insert some debugging statements in the program to print records as they are read or written, or print the data in intermediate stages as it is processed by the program. Be careful in printing because you can print hundreds of pages and have your job terminated before you get to the condition causing the error. You can avoid this by selectively printing the debugging information. Use IF statements to test for data or conditions that pinpoint the error. At worst you can count input records and begin printing debugging information only after so many records have been read.

In adding the debugging statements, you will, of course, make some errors and have to debug them first. Then you must make some debugging runs. If you do not have test data that produces the error, you must run the production data. Naturally the error will have occurred three hours into the run so that debugging is going to take a long time, assuming that you can even get your runs scheduled.

In short, you are in trouble. You must locate the error before you can correct it. Undoubtedly there will be a tight schedule with other systems depending on the output of the failing program. You may rush things and make some compounding errors. At this time it gets very lonely. Try to get some help. You need moral support if nothing else, but it is also good to have someone else to listen to your ideas, and you also need someone to help you check your work so you do not waste debugging runs. Do not get so immersed in the error that you fail to notify the proper people that the schedule has just gone to pieces. Notify them as soon as possible. Delay always makes matters worse.

You can prevent this kind of nightmare by anticipating it. Debugging aids are built into programs at the wrong time—during the program's development when errors are not a serious problem. They may be frequent, but they are not serious. After development the debugging aids are studiously removed from the production program to make it more efficient. But during production, errors are a very serious matter. They can cost you your job, and nothing is more serious than this. So just when you encounter a critical error that must be corrected immediately, you are left with no debugging tools.

Production programs need debugging aids too. You can include statements in the program to print the contents of each record as it is read or written, but have them activated by a run parameter. This way they are always there when you need them for debugging runs, but they produce no output during normal production runs.

However, the goal is to locate the cause of errors without debugging runs. If the program runs to completion and you cannot locate the error with file dumps, you may have no recourse. But if the program abnormally terminates, you can use the facilities of the operating system to supply you the information you need. Some compilers have an option to notify you of the source statement being executed when the program terminates, and a few also print the last record transmitted in each open file. You can also get an abnormal termination dump. It is a last resort and may be seldom used, but when a program abnormally terminates, you want all the information you can get. All of these items cost little in program efficiency and should be requested in all production jobs. Besides, what is a little program efficiency compared to job security?

Correcting Errors   After having located the cause, you must isolate the error. That is, you must be able to produce the error in some manner, preferably with test data, so that you can know when you have corrected it. Often you may not have test data or the time to prepare it. You will have the production data that caused the error, and it may be expedient to rerun the program with the production data. This saves time in preparing the test data, and if the program runs correctly, the system can proceed.

Correcting an error is similar to making a planned program change, except that your first goal is to get the program running correctly, and documentation may be deferred. Correcting errors is the one place where short cuts are excusable. If the company president expects to have your report along on a midday flight to a board of director's meeting, you may be forgiven for not scheduling a structured walkthrough to analyze your correction to the program. Once the error is corrected and the system running, you must go back and tidy up the documentation and make a clean job of it.

Index

BEYOND COBOL